Not for Circulation

Not for Circulation: The George E. Bogaars Story

Bertha Henson

RIDGE BOOKS
SINGAPORE

© 2022 Bertha Henson

Published under the Ridge Books imprint by:

NUS Press
National University of Singapore
AS3-01-02, 3 Arts Link
Singapore 117569

Fax: (65) 6774-0652
E-mail: nusbooks@nus.edu.sg
Website: http://nuspress.nus.edu.sg

ISBN: 978-981-325-162-5

National Library Board, Singapore Cataloguing in Publication Data
Name(s): Henson, Bertha.
Title: Not for circulation : the George E. Bogaars story / Bertha Henson.
Description: Singapore : NUS Press, [2021]
Identifier(s): ISBN 978-981-325-162-5
Subject(s): LCSH: Bogaars, George E. -1992. | Singapore--Officials and
    employees--Biography. | Civil service--Singapore--History.
Classification: DDC 352.63092--dc23

Cover Image: GEB inspecting a guard of honour formed by the Singapore Naval Volunteer Force, 1967.

Typeset by: Ogma Solutions Pvt Ltd
Printed by: Markono Print Media Pte Ltd

Table of Contents

Preface

On 25 October 2021, George Edwin Bogaars—GEB, to his many friends and colleagues in the Singapore Civil Service—would have been 95 years old. He died 29 years ago, in 1992. His name is better known to the Singapore Eurasian community and the older generation of civil servants than to the public at large. It's a pity. The men and women who worked for this pioneering civil servant extraordinaire thought that he deserved to be lauded for his role in building the Singapore story, which he started doing from the colonial days. Those were days fraught with personal danger and fractious politics, requiring a keen mind and a courageous heart to take Singapore through its birth pains and start its fledgling nationhood. Bogaars was both a spectator and a player at major milestones during this transition period.

One of the country's earliest heads of Civil Service, he was the all-round top civil servant, one who could claim to have a hand in building the country's financial, diplomatic, security and corporate infrastructure. Unlike other Civil Service pioneers, he was sucked into the heart of controversy in the years leading up to Singapore's independence in 1965. He headed the Special Branch, which arrested the communists and pro-communists in the 1960s. He reported directly to pioneer leaders such as Lee Kuan Yew and Goh Keng Swee, before they became political icons. He started the Singapore

Armed Forces from scratch when he was Permanent Secretary of Interior and Defence (the precursor of Home Affairs and Defence ministries). He was the head of the Civil Service, with a finger in a dozen or so Government-linked companies, attempting to shore up the country's infrastructure and expand its business portfolio. He held the country's purse strings when he moved into the Finance Ministry before his retirement on 31 October 1981 at age 55. His impressive resume belies a colourful, flamboyant character with a wicked sense of humour that he is much remembered for.

GEB was not a typical bureaucrat. He was neither civil nor servile. He was hearty, sociable and not beyond giving senior civil servants a tongue-lashing when he thought he should rein in their ambitions, especially their calls on the public purse. His language could be colourful, which disconcerted the puritanical and straight-laced. Even today, ex-subordinates recall him as someone who was larger than life, who maintained his bonhomie even in the last ten years of his life as an invalid laid low by a series of strokes. He bowed out of public life after a particularly difficult time in Keppel Corporation in 1984, where he was non-executive chairman, and almost immediately succumbed to a series of strokes that left him paralysed and incapable of speaking for the last ten years of his life. He died in 1992, at the age 65, leaving behind two daughters and a son. Goh Keng Swee, former cabinet minister and economic architect of modern Singapore, sent the family a wreath thanking GEB for his "great contribution to Singapore".

This memoir is based on George Edwin Bogaars' oral history recordings, the parts which he decided to leave for public consumption. He directed the National Archives to keep the rest of his history in the Civil Service private. His story is pieced together from his recordings, essays and media interviews, declassified material from the British and other national archives, journals on defence and public administration as well as interviews with his family, friends and those who had worked with him closely.

This memoir is an initiative by the Treasury Coffee Club (TCC) to commemorate the 95th birth anniversary of GEB on 25 October 2021. In his final tour of duty at the Treasury, as the Finance Ministry is traditionally called by insiders, GEB set up the TCC so that senior officers would spend their morning coffee break interacting with colleagues, discussing common work problems, and reflecting on the latest developments. While the coffeeclub located at the staff lounge of the Treasury's former premises at the CPF Building is no more, its spirit of informal exchange among colleagues and friends of information and points of view has continued over the decades. Pre-pandemic, members met for lunch bi-monthly.

Interactions more recently have been restricted to e-mail and WhatsApp exchanges and, during one of these, Herman Ronald Hochstadt ("hrh"), GEB's successor as the Permanent Secretary of the Treasury and patron of the TCC, suggested, and members readily agreed, that TCC commission a biography of GEB to be launched on GEB's 95th birth anniversary.

TCC members, as well as other former colleagues and friends of GEB, have contributed generously to defray the cost of producing this biography, reflecting the high esteem with which they continue to this day to regard their "Greatest Ever Boss". Keppel Corporation, through its Keppel Care Foundation, has also provided generous financial support for the project, in recognition of GEB's services to Singapore as one of the foremost public and corporate sector leaders of the Pioneer Generation, and for setting the long-term vision that has guided Keppel's development to this day. The full list of those who have contributed financially to cover the cost of the project is at the end of the book.

Proceeds from the sale of this book will be credited to an endowment fund at the National University of Singapore (NUS) recognising top performing students of the History Department. GEB himself was such a top performer, being one of the first two students to be awarded a Master of Arts by NUS's predecessor institution, the University of Malaya, in 1952.

Timeline

1926: George Edwin Bogaars was born on 25 October
1933: Studied at St Patrick's School
1942: Start of Japanese Occupation in Singapore (March)
1943: Moved to Bahau, Negeri Sembilan, in Malaysia (December)
1945: End of Japanese Occupation (August); Moved back to Singapore (November)
1946: Studied at St Joseph's Institution
1947: Undergraduate studies at Raffles College
1950: Attained his general degree
1952: Attained BA (Honours) in History and Master's from the University of Malaya; Started work at the Ministry of Trade and Commerce as an Administrative Service Part II officer
1954: Married Dorothy Lee Kian Neo (October)
1955: Started work at the Treasury; David Marshall of Labour Front became Singapore's first Chief Minister (April)
1957: His first daughter, Paulina, was born
1959: The People's Action Party won the general election and became the Government
1960: Promoted to Deputy Secretary Grade G
1961: Promoted to Deputy Secretary Grade E; Appointed as Director of the Special Branch under the Ministry of Home Affairs (August)
1962: Awarded the Meritorious Service Medal
1963: Under his directorship, Operation Coldstore was conducted (February); Singapore became part of Malaysia (September)

1964: His second daughter, Christina, was born

1965: Singapore became an independent country; Promoted to Permanent Secretary Grade C; Became Permanent Secretary at the Ministry of Interior and Defence (later Ministry of Defence); Awarded the Malaysia Medal

1966: His son, George Michael, was born

1967: Awarded the Distinguished Service Order

1968: Became the Head of Civil Service

1969: Promoted to Permanent Secretary Grade A

1970: Became Permanent Secretary at the Ministry of Finance, Economic Development Division; Became Chairman of Keppel Corporation

1972: Became Permanent Secretary at the Ministry of Foreign Affairs; Awarded Honorary Doctor of Letters (University of Singapore)

1975: Became Permanent Secretary at the Ministry of Finance, Budget Division

1977: Divorced from his wife (February)

1980: Became Chairman of Far East Levingston Limited; Suffered his first heart attack

1981: Retired from the Civil Service; Became Chairman of National Iron and Steel Mills Limited

1983: Became Chairman of Straits Steamship Company Limited; Keppel acquired 82 per cent of Straits Steamship Company at $408 million, which was then the biggest corporate takeover in Singapore's history

1984: Relinquished his chairmanship of Keppel Corporation; Suffered his first stroke in December

1985: Relinquished his chairmanship of National Iron and Steel Mills Limited; Suffered a second stroke in March and a third in October, which had him hospitalised for 15 months

1992: George Edwin Bogaars died of heart failure on 6 April

I

A Teenager in Wartime Singapore

The bayonet was pointed at his stomach. George thought he would surely die. He flung up his arms to expose the bread loaves that he was holding and indicated that he was just getting into his own house. He wasn't stealing or up to no good. The Japanese soldier, somewhat mollified, said, "Go in, go in," and that was when George realised that he wasn't going to suffer the fate of so many Chinese men he had seen over the past months, tied to a lamp post, or worse, eviscerated or decapitated.

It was a routine errand that almost went wrong. That morning, on hearing news that a bakery at Sungei Road had started operating, his parents sent him and his younger brother, Brian, to get some bread. It would add to their usual diet of tinned corned beef. But the brothers got separated somehow on their way home. Brian managed to get into the back door of the shophouse-cum-clinic in Victoria Street first. But George came face to face with the Japanese soldier who suddenly appeared out of nowhere.

In 1942, when the British surrendered Singapore to the Imperial Japanese Army, George Edwin Bogaars was just 15. His brother Brian was 13, while sister Patricia was 18.

Early days

The man who had more than a ringside seat in Singapore's tumultuous history was a Katong boy. He attended preschool classes at the Convent of the Holy Infant Jesus in Martia Road before moving to St Patrick's School when it was ready to take in students in 1933.

But once the bombings started, life for GEB (as he was known to his friends and colleagues in his adult life) changed. Those years of hardship, including a two-year stay in the Bahau settlement in Negeri Sembilan during the Japanese Occupation, instilled in him a sense of mission and a stake in the future of a fledgling Singapore.

The GEB story isn't a rags-to-riches fairy tale. He had a privileged upbringing. The Bogaarses could be described as an upper middle-class family who belonged to the "Upper Ten" of Eurasian society, despite being darker-complexioned than most Eurasians of European descent.

Grandfather George Edward Bogaars, who moved to Singapore from Ceylon in 1906, was a local luminary, having set up the *Malaya Tribune*, first in Malacca and, later, in Singapore. He was what is known as a Dutch Burgher, tracing his ancestry to the Netherlands but with a mix of Portuguese, Tamil or Sinhalese in the bloodline.

Besides a sprawling attap-roofed bungalow in St Francis Road in Serangoon, where many Ceylonese Eurasians lived, he had holiday homes in Pasir Ris and Frankel Estate. When he died in 1941, before the bombing of Singapore, a roll call of who's who in the Eurasian community turned up for his funeral at the Bidadari Cemetery. There was Mr G. S. Hammonds, who represented the Tribune group of newspapers. There were the Tessensohns, the de Souzas, the Oehlers, the Cockburns, the da Silvas, the Woodfords, the Westerhouts, the Norrises and the Martens, to name a few Eurasian clans.

GEB's father, George Edward Bogaars (named after Grandfather Bogaars), was already serving in the British colonial government by the time of his son's birth in 1926. During the colonial period, many Eurasians held white-collar jobs and were employed as clerks in the Civil Service, European banks, commercial and trading houses. A substantial number of Eurasian women also worked, mainly as teachers and nurses. The 1931 census records listed 6,900 Eurasians living in Singapore at that time. This went up to 8,145 in 1940, according to *The Straits Times*. The Eurasians had an economic advantage over the other ethnic communities in colonial Singapore because of their fluency in English, as well as their familiarity with the habits and customs of the British.

GEB Senior's excellent stenographic skills would land him the job of confidential secretary to not just one, but four colonial governors. He accompanied them on train tours in Malaya and was in the confidence of British administrators such as Sir Cecil Clementi Smith, Governor of the Straits Settlements from 1930 to 1934, who would dictate dispatches to him for forwarding to the colonial secretariat in London.

In 1922, he had married Edwina Tessensohn at the Cathedral of the Good Shepherd, in what was a nod to the bride's side, who were Roman Catholics. The couple moved into the maternal family's home in Amber Road, a large two-storey compound house in which the dining room alone could hold 40 people. They had a driver, a cook, a "kitchen boy" and two maids. The Tessensohns were an illustrious family, with a road named after them.

In letters to his daughters late in his life, GEB recalled the pranks and activities he and his brother as well as their cousins got up to, like jumping off from the top of the stairs in the house, picnicking at Katong Park on Saturdays and the magnificent Christmas parties with two or three turkeys and "very large" chicken pies baked for family members who would gather in the house.

Then the nuclear families in the house started peeling off to set up their own homes. To be near their schools, GEB's family moved to a single-storey bungalow in St Patrick's Road, surrounded by a garden filled with fruit trees like chiku, jambu, coconut, jamun and carambola (starfruit). They had a driver, a cook, a maid and a handyman who lived in the servants' quarters in the compound. Many rich Chinese families had their homes in the area. They became close to a Chinese family surnamed Ong, who later helped them out by sending them bags of rice during the Japanese Occupation.

Comfortable quarters didn't mean a soft upbringing. GEB Senior was an autocratic disciplinarian who abhorred laziness. There was a chicken run at the house which became the responsibility of his two sons. They had to feed the fowl twice a day, in the mornings and evenings, whether it was a school day or not. From just a dozen chicks, the flock grew to more than a hundred in three years. He made his sons wear pith helmets to school, which earned them a lot of teasing and torment. His name was invoked by neighbours to put the fear of God into their children.

GEB Senior's resourcefulness and frugality stood the family in good stead when the deprivations of the Japanese Occupation started to affect the residents. He had savings, including an advance in salary paid to civil servants—and he wasn't above dabbling in black market transactions to feed his family.

Bombing starts

In the early hours of 8 December 1941, George was woken from sleep by what he thought was thunder. The whole family was roused by the noise and had gathered in the garden. They could see that their neighbours were up as well. Everyone was looking up at the clear night sky. The stars were out. And it didn't look like anything untoward was happening. Then a siren wailed. And stopped. Wailed. And stopped. GEB Senior, more attuned to happenings around the world, used the house telephone to ring his official contacts for information. Putting the phone down, he told his family matter-of-factly: "Oh, you know, Singapore is being bombed."

The Imperial Japanese Navy Air Service had sent 17 aircraft from Saigon in Vietnam to attack Singapore's Seletar and Tengah air bases. Japanese bombs struck a number of targets across the island, including Chinatown, killing 61 people and injuring another 133 people. Like the Bogaarses, many people had turned out on the streets after hearing the explosions, thinking it was another air raid exercise. It was a fatal move for some.

As a teenager, George hadn't been too interested in news of Japanese depredations in Indochina or the German Nazi onslaught in Europe. His father did not discuss such matters with the children. But there were signs that everyone was getting tetchy, in the conversations he overheard, or in news reports of attacks on Japanese shops. There was Echigoya, a Japanese shop in Middle Road which had its window panes broken and goods, mainly textiles, tarred. It stuck in his memory because the shop had a toy department and his mother had brought him there to shop for Christmas gifts. There was also a Japanese community of fishermen, further down the coast where St Patrick's School was. He had heard them being described as spies. Still, the teenager didn't think anything of it. He only remembered an old Japanese fisherman who spent his evenings selling delicious red-bean cakes on his tricycle.

As far as he could tell, there were no signs of panic that the Japanese would be heading to Singapore. Civil defence preparedness amounted to equipping families with a stirrup pump to put out fires.

"Pathetic" was the word GEB used in his oral interview recorded for the national archives. Even when the first bombs started dropping, Singapore was still ablaze with lights, despite the sirens. It transpired that the operator of the lighting switchboard was in a cinema and had taken the keys with him.

After the bombing, GEB Senior and his superiors decided that the family should move to a house in Chancery Lane, near Government House (today's Istana) where he worked. Also, the conventional wisdom at that time was that the Japanese would land on the east coast, which would not be a place for any family to be. The Bogaarses could have left Singapore, like George's maternal grandmother and aunt did, before the Japanese over-ran the country. But GEB Senior decided that his own family should stay put, perhaps out of loyalty or the fear of dislocation.

Most Eurasians and not a few Chinese were convinced that the British would be able to hold out, trusting the propaganda that Singapore was an impregnable fortress. The Japanese were often derided as short people with bad teeth, good at copying other people's products like textiles and toys. Like many others resident in Singapore, GEB Senior reckoned that it would be a matter of weeks before the British pushed the Japanese back into the sea. GEB said in his oral history recordings that those in his father's generation were in shock when the British surrendered: "How could this type of people, how could they defeat a European power like the British, a western power like the British?"

Anyway, for a week or so that December, there was some frantic packing of belongings, and multiple trips in cars to Chancery Lane— along with the 100 or so chickens, turkeys, ducks and geese. The house was a black-and-white bungalow raised above the ground. Besides the Bogaarses, GEB's maternal aunt Freda, her husband Dr William Balhetchet and their four children moved in as well.

GEB Senior continued going to work as usual, until a bomb landed on the grounds of Government House.

That morning in January or February, he was getting his usual lift to work from Dr Balhetchet, who had a Red Cross on his car which allowed him to cross into restricted areas. When the sirens sounded, the two men had no time to get out of the car, recalled Dr Balhetchet's daughter, Sheila, in her oral history reminiscences. Shrapnel from the bomb went through the windscreen, leaving GEB Senior with splinters and a damaged ear. They drove to Singapore General Hospital to get him stitched up. GEB himself recalled that his mother was frantic, telling her husband to stop going to work. GEB Senior would have continued, except that the British office decided that local employees should not be put at risk. He was told to stay home, but took off on his bicycle every day to meet friends to exchange news.

At Chancery Lane, the brothers were put to work tending the chicken run—until Christmas Day. On returning home from a Christmas party, the family found that they had been robbed of all their poultry. Then the brothers and a cousin threw their energies into building an air raid shelter behind the house, which backed into Oldham Hill. They cut into the hill, supported the roof with beams and dug out a cavern big enough to hold 14 people. Benches were put in. GEB recalled that it was used only a few times, until the bombs were being dropped daily. These attacks became so frequent that he had to ditch his attempt to keep a record of every bombing spree.

The bombings intensified in January 1942 with two to three attacks daily, each carried out by groups of 27 or 54 Japanese aircraft. The Royal Air Force found that their F2A Buffalo planes were outmatched by Japanese Zero fighters, and the Hurricane MKIIs that arrived later were also unable to secure British control of the skies. By February, the Japanese had taken control of Johor and were sending a barrage of artillery fire into Singapore. "That was a nerve-wracking experience. Because [with] bombing, you could hear the planes and more or less you knew [that] if you didn't hear the whine of the bomb, you knew you were safe. The shells, they came from you didn't know where," GEB recalled.

His brother and a cousin went on their bicycles to the Newton area which they heard had been bombed to bits. They saw a man who was hugging a tree; he had no head. Traumatised by what they had seen, the boys lost their appetite that day.

More and more Australian soldiers were also turning up in Singapore, as they made their retreat from Johor. They carried with them tales of Japanese atrocities exacted on the Chinese population. Those in the Eurasian community wondered if the Japanese would treat them more like the Europeans than the Chinese—bad but not so bad. Or would torture them to death because they were suspected to be in cahoots with the British. Then an Australian officer turned up at the house, suggesting that they leave the premises because they were placing an artillery battery in the front garden to face the Japanese, who were coming down Bukit Timah Road.

GEB Senior decided to uproot the family again, this time to the Singapore General Hospital where Dr Balhetchet had secured living quarters. It was like a refugee camp with people crammed into a few rooms. Worse, the Japanese believed that the hospital was being used as a cover for military activities and it was subjected to constant bombing. After just four or five days, the family decamped. They had no choice. Bombs had been dropped in front of, and behind, the living quarters.

Then the unthinkable happened. On 8 February 1942, Japanese soldiers cycled their way into Singapore via the Causeway. A week later, something even more unthinkable happened: The British surrendered Singapore.

Under Occupation

On the morning of 15 February, Lieutenant-General Arthur Ernest Percival, the General Officer Commanding for Malaya, and Sir Shenton Thomas, the colonial Governor, met the British military commanders at the Fort Canning Bunker (now known as the Battle Box)—and decided to throw in the towel. The situation was dire. With water pipes damaged, Singapore had only enough water to last one day. The Japanese had also taken over the reservoirs. Later that day, Percival and his surrender party met Lieutenant-General Tomoyuki Yamashita in the Japanese headquarters located at the Ford Factory in Bukit Timah and officially surrendered Singapore to the Japanese 25th Army.

By then, the Bogaarses had moved to the second floor of a clinic called Sin Chew Hospital at the junction of Arab Street and Victoria Street. A Tessensohn uncle and his Scottish-born wife lived there with their three children. The Bogaarses had two rooms to themselves. Their lodgings gave them a vantage view of the goings-on in the area. They were right outside a cordoned-off area encompassing North Bridge Road and Rochor Road, Rochor Canal Road and Lavender Street. It looked like the setting of a concentration camp; barbed wire surrounded the perimeter. Male Chinese, young and old, mingled outside the perimeter for their turn to be "registered".

What George didn't know then was that Operation Sook Ching was in progress. Male Chinese were being called up. With the help of hooded informers, several screening stations had been set up in the urban areas, especially in Chinatown, to weed out "anti-Japanese elements". It was an indiscriminate process dependent on the whims and fancies of the assigned Japanese officer. The men who were fortunate enough to pass the screening process were allowed to leave the centres. They were provided with a piece of paper with a stamp that said "examined", or had the stamps marked on their face, arm, shoulder or clothing. But thousands of others were not so fortunate. They were loaded into lorries and transported to remote areas such as Changi, Punggol and Bedok, and machine-gunned to death. Often, their bodies were thrown into the sea. The operation lasted ten days and ended in early March. The Japanese estimated that there were between 5,000 and 6,000 executions, while the local Chinese put the number between 40,000 and 50,000 (which may have included those killed by shelling and bombardment during the Malaya Campaign). The true numbers are unlikely ever to be known.

From his window, George could see that buildings and houses in the area were locked and empty. The Chinese men just lived on the streets. Occasionally, lorries would pull out of the area to take a load of them somewhere. These were the times when a few brave souls took the opportunity to run away. "We used to hear gun shooting. And then [we] looked out of the window and we saw a fellow fall on his face, being shot by a Japanese guard," he recalled.

In April, it was the Eurasians' turn to be "registered". They were called to the Singapore Recreation Club at the Padang and given numbered tickets. Queues formed in front of tables where Japanese soldiers were taking down details, helped by a few Eurasians. There was apprehension all round as the people wondered if they would be interned somewhere or allowed to leave. By this time, the fate of the thousands of Chinese men rounded up in Operation Sook Ching had become common knowledge.

> All of us were given a little slip of paper. And then my father and some of his very close friends disappeared. They told us, "Stay where you are." They went off and I don't know what happened. They went off for quite a considerable length of time and then came back after some hours and then told us, "Okay, we can all go home."

The Japanese had been trying to sort the Eurasians into different categories, such as those of European parentage and local Eurasians who were born here. It was an arbitrary arrangement which depended on the answers to questions, fairness of complexion and a couple of Eurasians standing by who were helping the Japanese. Some were taken away for internment at Changi Prison immediately. Others were given a red badge with a white star and told to report every week at the police station. The rest, like the Bogaarses, could go home. GEB figured that his father must have told the Japanese that his father was born in Ceylon and had made every attempt to prove that he was not of European parentage.

Over time, the "starred" Eurasians would find themselves rounded up from their homes and interned in Changi Prison. The Scottish wife of the uncle who had put up the Bogaarses was given the red badge. Asked if she wanted to leave her three children behind with her husband, she said she wanted them with her. This was a common practice. Internment was a better option than scrabbling for a living on the outside. Children received extra rations and the women would not have to suffer the sexual advances of predatory men on the lawless streets. The interned Eurasians were moved from Changi Prison to the Sime Road camp from 1944. Male Eurasians, by September 1945, numbered 459 of the 4,507 civilian internees. There were also 299 Eurasian women who were incarcerated, according to *The Straits Times*.

Most of the Eurasians who formed the machine gun regiment of the Singapore Voluntary Corps also turned up to register, because they had been told that they would be interned instead of executed. For four or five Sundays, the Bogaars boys, accompanying their Catholic mother, would run into these men when they went for mass at the St Joseph's Church along Victoria Street. "We used to see them and talk to them and all that, pass them food and the rest of it. And the Japanese were fairly kind of relaxed to them." Then they stopped appearing. An escapee from Changi Prison told the

Bogaars family that close to 100 of them had been machine-gunned on the beach.

By the middle of 1942, the family had moved back into the Chancery Lane house. GEB Senior thought it better to leave the Victoria Street area where so much of the "action" was taking place. The lamp post outside the house, for example, was being used for disciplining recalcitrant Chinese who had somehow angered the Japanese sentries when they passed by. They were tied in a squatting or kneeling position for the whole day before a guard would release them. Recalled GEB: "And then he would stagger off, sunburnt and very ill…. So we used to see lots of these kinds of incidents, shooting of people trying to escape from this enclosure."

The Chancery Lane house, however, was a shambles with broken furniture and rubbish strewn everywhere. There were grenades, bullets, pistols and decomposing food. After the Bogaarses left the premises, the retreating Australian soldiers had used the house as a base to launch artillery attacks. For one week, the family shuttled to and from Victoria Street and Chancery Lane to get the house in order. If they thought being on the move would help them avoid Japanese attention, they were mistaken.

Living on the edge

One day, Japanese Kempeitai officers came knocking on the Chancery Lane door to speak to GEB Senior. They took him away with them. "We thought this was the end, we would never see him again. In the evening, he came back," said GEB.

Every morning for a week to ten days, GEB Senior would walk to the Kempeitai headquarters in Stamford Road, where the YMCA now stands. "We always thought that that was the last we would see of the chap. But he came back every evening."

GEB Senior told the family that he had to write "essays", which George took to mean information about his work. One evening, a car dropped him off at the house—and that marked the last of his daily trips. GEB found out later that his father had outwitted the Japanese into believing that he was just a low-ranking clerk when in fact, he was among the rarefied ranks of colonial bureaucracy privy to high-level official correspondence.

In the meantime, George and his brother decided that they should start filching what they could from the empty houses in the largely European residences in Scotts Road and Gilstead Road. The Bogaarses' own furnishings had started dwindling. The Japanese were entering the house and buying furniture for their own use. It wasn't polite to say no. GEB Senior was also making some money selling off bits and pieces of furniture, including a piano, to a Chinese racketeer who operated in Sungei Road. One item, a Tudor lamp the Bogaars boys had stolen, went for 1,500 Japanese dollars.

> My father was a fairly thrifty man. So we had quite a bit of money, British currency, which was very valuable because it exchanged at fantastic rates for Japanese notes. And then all sorts of other things, personal effects and all the rest of it, which gradually we sold and disposed of. For quite some time, things were fairly cheap until the impact of Japanese Occupation took place and then prices began to move up and up.

In September 1944, a dollar in Malayan currency was exchanged for $14 in the Japanese currency, locally known as "banana money". Retailers who were appointed agents for the distribution of rice, sugar and cigarettes during the Occupation weren't beyond short-changing those who came with their green ration cards to collect their share. People hoarded precious commodities and sold them for a profit. By the time the Japanese Occupation ended, a pikul (about 60.5 kg) of rice went up from $5 in Malayan currency (or $70 in banana money) to $5,000 in Malayan currency, while a dozen eggs cost $120 in Malayan currency, up from 24 Malayan cents.

In such circumstances, people gravitated to the black market. "We ourselves black marketed some of the things … cigarettes for instance. My father was the only one who smoked. And so he cut down his smoking. And with the balance, we black-marketed," GEB recalled.

While the Japanese closed one eye to these shenanigans, they were tough on looters.

> They beheaded a few looters … six or something like that and stuck their heads on various places, Fullerton Bridge and outside the Cathay cinema. I didn't see any of these heads. But one of my cousins … went round having a look at these things on their bicycles. And they said they were very gruesome. So it was that kind of law by the sword, I think.

That was when the brothers' looting spree ended. "My parents wouldn't let us do it."

Towards the end of the year, the Bogaars boys made friends with a Japanese second lieutenant who had inadvertently lost his footing and tumbled down the hill into their Chancery Lane backyard.

> He became very friendly with my brother and I. Because we were roughly about the same age. He may have been a year or two older than us. He could speak halting English. We knew no Japanese at that time. And we kind of spoke, had a conversation, he gave me lots of Japanese coins which he had and stamps and things like that. It was a kind of, you know, a schoolboy's friendship. … So here was a young fellow whom I met who was very friendly, almost thinking and behaving like us. I realised in the end there were people among them who were good and there were people among them who were bad.

That's when the family discovered that members of a Japanese tank unit had parked themselves on the nearby hill. Worried for his daughter's safety, GEB Senior and family moved again, this time to Grandpa Bogaars' old house at St Francis Road. A community of Eurasians lived in this upper-class Serangoon area, crisscrossed by streets with the names of saints like St George, St Wilfred, St Lawrence and St Michael.

Because GEB Senior didn't want them to enrol in schools which were under Japanese control, he kept the boys busy learning shorthand, tending to the newly replenished chicken run and doing the weekly marketing.

In the first year of the Occupation, there were still plenty of vegetables, fish, chicken, beef and pork, which the boys bought at a wet market on Idris Road about two to three kilometres away. On occasion, rice sacks came from the Ongs, former neighbours who somehow always had a plentiful supply.

The teenagers learnt simple survival skills while going about their chores, like making sure they avoided Japanese sentries on their rounds or getting off their bicycles to bow if they ran into one. Nobody wanted a slap on the face—or worse. There was also talk that the Koreans who had been drafted by the Japanese were the most brutal.

It was living life on a precipice.

George recalled how his mother took the two boys for an early morning mass at St Joseph's Church when they were suddenly confronted by two Japanese sentries with pistols drawn. "My mother was talking to them. She told us, 'You go on walking ahead,' and they didn't mind. Later on, when she joined us, she said, 'Oh, they are policemen.' So I presumed they were checking people who were out early in the morning."

Talk at the time was all about informers and collaborators. Fingers were pointed at those who appeared to be too friendly with the Japanese or who were tipping them off about who was breaking the rules. Informers were considered less perfidious than the collaborators who worked actively with the Japanese to keep law and order in the colony.

The Bogaarses had every reason to be wary of informers. GEB Senior had a radio in the house which he used to listen to the BBC. The radio was tucked at the bottom of a clothes basket. The boys stood guard outside the house every time he switched it on. A Protestant pastor would sometimes come by to ask, "Any fish today?" The boys would reply, "Yes," which meant their father was listening in. And so he would join their father and both of them listened to the radio. The pastor, who had access to Changi Prison, would pass on snippets of news to the British prisoners-of-war.

The family had a shock one morning when an altercation broke out in the house next door, where some "starred" Eurasians lived. The Japanese were raiding the house because an informer had told them, wrongly, that the residents were listening to the radio. "If they'd come to our house, they would have found the radio … I mean, it was just in a clothes basket and with clothes on the top." That morning, the family packed the radio into a steel trunk—and buried it in their chicken run.

This was also one of the reasons GEB Senior decided that the family should leave Singapore.

II

"Escape" to Bahau

For the past few months, GEB Senior had been making plans to uproot his family. Singapore had become too dangerous a place for them. Although a Protestant, he spent the free time he now had working as a volunteer in the Roman Catholic Archbishop's secretariat, sorting out administrative matters. That was how he got wind of the diocese's plans to settle some members of the Catholic and Eurasian communities up north in the jungles of Malaya.

Some of his relatives and friends were against it, suggesting that the family bide its time in Singapore. The belief that the war would soon be over with the British emerging victorious was deeply held. But GEB Senior had had enough of close shaves with the Japanese Kempeitai. He decided that the two brothers would leave first, as the vanguard for the family and clear the way, so to speak. It spoke volumes of his confidence in the two teenagers that he packed them onto a train for Bahau in Negeri Sembilan in December 1943. They belonged to only the second batch of settlers so far.

George and Brian took matters in their stride. It was not in them to question their father. They did not know that this was part of a "self-sufficiency" programme that the Eurasian and Catholic communities had proposed to the Japanese to deal with the food shortages forced by the Allied forces' blockade of the port. Rice and sugar were scarce and Singapore was running out of all sorts of provisions.

A Chinese settlement had already been established in Endau in Johor and glowing reports of living conditions had been filtering back to Singapore. What the Bahau early settlers seemed to have overlooked was that Endau was much closer to Singapore and any necessities could be easily ferried across. It was also well supported by the Overseas Chinese Association, which gave $1 million as start-up costs. Bahau, on the other hand, was nestled in the jungle, dependent on the authorities in Negeri Sembilan, and required a 24-hour train journey from Singapore. The settlement was eight kilometres away from Bahau town.

Bishop Adrien Devals, as well as representatives of the Eurasian community in Singapore, had visited Bahau to assess its suitability. They had a patron in former Japanese diplomat Mamoru Shinozaki, who played a big role in the Bahau project as a middleman between the settlers and the Japanese authorities. Although there were some qualms about the suitability of the land and its red clay soil for planting crops, the Eurasians desperately wanted out. They were terrified of the close watch that the Japanese Kempeitai was keeping on them.

The Japanese okayed the plan and called the area Fuji-Go. *The Syonan Shimbun*, the English-language Japanese-run newspaper in Singapore, talked up the project and praised its achievements. But the truth was that many Eurasians lost their lives in the mosquito-infested jungle, food provisions were not always enough and medical care was scant.

The 8,500 acres of land was divided into two segments. The Bogaarses were sent to Mukim Five, which also had a large community of Chinese Catholics. There was also Mukim Six, which harboured only Eurasians. Between December 1943 and April 1944, some 2,000 Eurasians in Singapore left their homes for Bahau, joined by the Chinese Roman Catholics and a group of Protestant Europeans. With their personal belongings and some books, the two teenagers got onto a train carriage with facing seats for their first trip out of the country. They were the youngest of the 50 or so people who boarded the train. They knew no one.

The ride proved uneventful and they spent most of their time nodding off. It was a different matter when they reached the Bahau train station. A welcoming party, or what looked to them like one, was waiting for the new settlers. They were among the first batch of settlers, all men, and the brothers were soon to find out that they were there to receive packages or baggage that their own families in Singapore had sent up.

With their belongings loaded onto trucks, the boys were on their way to the place they would call home for the next two years. "We went at a very bad time of the year when it was raining quite heavily in Bahau. And the roads were just kind of wide avenues cut into the jungles. Very slimy and muddy and slushy when it rains. So it was quite an effort to move around," GEB recalled in his oral history recordings.

When the terrain proved too tough for the trucks, they got off, lugging their belongings through thick curtains of green and stepping on logs that doubled as bridges. Evidently the "settlement" was not yet ready for settling in.

The boys soon realised why only men, mainly bachelors, had been sent up first. Although the trees had been felled, the contracted local loggers had left the debris behind. The backbreaking work of clearing them, cutting out the roads and building bridges had yet to be done.

As for accommodation, what confronted them were two long communal houses with attap roofs held up by poles. Inside, a wide raised bench, commonly known as *balik balik*, ran through the middle of the house, serving as their beds. Mosquito nets hung down from the roof. Accommodation was just a matter of finding a free space on the clay-packed floor and setting down your belongings. "The first thing you want to know, of course, [is] where were the toilets? And then we were told that there were no toilets. You just go into the jungle and you do your business and then manage as best as you can." The sanitary pit was one critical piece of infrastructure that was not yet in place.

About ten La Salle Christian brothers were already in the camp, guiding newcomers on what to do, where to go and putting up work rosters. Over time, they would be joined by the Gabrielites and the Canossian nuns, who brought along with them about 100 orphans, mainly girls.

While the men had been set to clear the roads, the two teens found themselves assigned to work in the cookhouse, a separate shed surrounded by three huge cauldrons, for cooking rice, soup and vegetables. GEB recalled the set-up:

> There was a big hole in the ground and then a tunnel where you shoved your wood in. And then the fire came through the main hole under a ledge. It was built so that you can rest these very big cauldrons. They were very large cauldrons made of brass, about the biggest I've seen in my entire life. I haven't seen them again anywhere else.

The kitchen crew was up before everyone else in the morning, boiling rice, peeling sweet potatoes and making tea while waiting for the day's provisions to come down by truck. The specialty was "Evan's bouquet", named after the cook who dished out a vegetable soup with bits of meat floating in it. Nights were pretty convivial in the communal halls with singing and guitar playing and even talent contests.

But in the main, everyone was in a hurry to get their own accommodations set up quickly on the piece of land that they had been allotted. The boys had their three acre plot of land too, on the left side of the settlement. In the afternoons, they used parangs and axes to clear the area of vegetation. Hardier trees and stumps were simply set ablaze. By then, they had made some friends and land-clearing and home-building became a more collaborative effort. The boys learnt how to chop down trees, collect the thatching for the roof and how to strip rattan to tie pieces of wood together.

Back in Singapore, GEB Senior, who had a major role at the Bahau office in Singapore supervising the trips and the provisions, wasn't pleased with the progress of construction. He paid a local contractor $300 to finish the work for the boys. The one-storey wooden house partitioned into three rooms was laid with planed timber flooring and even had a veranda. It was raised from the earth, which meant that chickens could be kept under the house. A separate hut housed the kitchen, dining room and bathroom. It was easily the biggest house in the settlement and aroused a great deal of envy, according to Fiona Hodgkins in her interviews with Bahau settlers in her book, *From Syonan to Fuji-go*.

Living off the land

Bahau wasn't bereft of amenities. There were a few Malay villages nearby and Chinese stores near the train station. Trucks went to and fro, from the settlement to "town", ferrying people and provisions. The Singapore side had an arrangement with the Japanese to have their rations sent up to Bahau. The settlers could also buy what they needed from the stores or barter their personal belongings for rice, a commodity that was in short supply. Then there were the "packages" from home, which included curtains and pianos, sent by family members still in Singapore. GEB's mother, Edwina, sent up several loads of belongings, including a giant earthenware pot. "The thing was a nuisance. Because we had to manhandle it. My brother and I, just two of us carrying the thing for a couple of miles. It wasn't very funny at that time. In the end, it became useful. We used to fill it with water for bathing."

But comfortable furnishings counted for naught when it came to farming. The townsfolk from Singapore didn't have any experience growing crops. They didn't know, for example, that you had to dig a large hole the size of the seat of a chair to plant banana rhizomes and to fill the hole with burnt soil. They tried planting a strain of tapioca which took too long to mature. Help came in the form of local experts sent by the British to study agriculture during the pre-Occupation days. The two Chinese men introduced a fast-growing tapioca plant that matured in four months. As for the banana plants, the Bogaarses had about 200 planted in all.

GEB Senior retained his obsession with poultry. When he brought his wife and daughter to Bahau six months later, he took along six chickens from Singapore. His sons were back to their old drill, tending the chicken run. At one point, they had 200 or so chickens flapping around. The experience stuck with GEB who, in later years, would buy books on rearing chickens for his children to read.

Digging wells for water required expertise of a certain type as well. The brothers had dug a well which proved to be an unreliable source of water supply. Then, a Christian brother, who used a pocket watch as a water divining aid, pointed them to a different location to dig. Voila! There was water—except that the well was quite a distance away, which meant more backbreaking work lugging pails of water to the house.

The Bogaarses had it relatively easy compared to latecomers. While other Bahau settlers complained of the wretched conditions they were subjected to with disease and death surrounding them after they returned to Singapore, GEB was relatively positive about his experience.

> We were never short of things like sweet potatoes, tapioca, bananas, vegetables, eggs, poultry. Never, never short of that. We could manage somehow. The problem was rice and sugar. We couldn't grow rice and our land was too dry to grow rice. We tried. It didn't work. So we had to barter our shirts and things like that for rice and sugar.

The settlement soon grew enough of some types of food to trade with merchants in Singapore. GEB Senior was part of a group of men who formed a sort of co-operative, known as *kumiai*, to take care of the stores and liaise with their counterparts in Singapore. Trucks took produce into the country for sale and returned laden with much-needed provisions, like condensed milk and palm oil. But rice and sugar were still scarce commodities. Some months, rice would be mixed with red beans to provide adequate sustenance, recalled GEB.

Settlers who moved into plots near ravines had a better time farming because of the nearby streams and better soil. They grew rice and ragi. But those who had to contend with the red, clayish soil on hilly ground couldn't make their farms a going concern. Settlers in Mukim Six had to resort to eating rats and snails when their crops failed.

In his oral records, GEB said he thought that the pioneer batches comprised the better-off who somehow also received more fertile pieces of land. Because the family had savings and personal belongings, they could barter with the villagers for basic necessities. Those who settled later in Bahau were from the poorer strata of society and had been given more difficult terrain to farm. This class distinction became more apparent as the months went by. The latecomers ran out of money and had no personal possessions left to barter.

Fellow forest dwellers

Besides chicken, meat for the Bogaarses came in the form of jungle fowl, mousedeer, pheasants and wood pigeons that the brothers and their friends had trapped in the jungle. But such adventures weren't without hazards as wild animals such as panthers and elephants had their habitats there. The brothers never encountered them, although George was once chased by a water buffalo and bitten by a centipede, which put him out of action for a day. Tales abound of elephants which stuck their trunks into homes on the outskirts of the settlement.

Also in the jungle were Chinese guerrillas. One day, a Chinese man in his mid-20s appeared in the jungle clearing at the back of the Bogaarses' house and started talking to the brothers. He couldn't speak English but was fluent in Malay. The man, Lim, who was almost always clad in a white shirt and white shorts, popped up every week or so, mainly to have tea with the brothers and their friends. He also took them through the jungle, which he was clearly familiar with, naming the trees, pointing out areas which used to be inhabited and taking them to the best spots to fish.

The young people believed he was pro-British as he sometimes handed them English pamphlets reporting on the progress of the war. In hindsight, GEB believed he belonged to Force 136 set up by the British as a resistance force. His brother, Brian, didn't agree. He told Hodgkins in her book that he thought the man was a communist. The Malayan Communist Party, founded in 1930, had a resistance arm known as the Malayan People's Anti-Japanese Army to conduct guerrilla activities against the Japanese.

Evidently, Lim had been sent to find out who these settlers were and glean information about Japanese movements. But the youths had nothing to tell Lim and were content to keep their relationship social. GEB Senior didn't much like the brothers consorting with Lim but didn't forbid it either.

While Lim put in occasional appearances, the mosquitoes were a constant presence. The settlers were afflicted with mosquito-borne diseases such as malaria, which could affect the brain, induce a coma and cause death. Many settlers were laid low by malaria, some fatally. Some experienced more than 30 bouts of illness through their stay in Bahau. To combat malaria, quinine was distributed and ingested before the onset of malaria season. But the effects of quinine were too much for some, as it induced a kind of out-of-body experience. Some, like George, decided not to take the drug—to their regret. When he contracted malaria, he was so delirious that his mother had to tie him to his bed.

Medical help was practically non-existent. There was a small clinic-cum-dispensary manned by a former nurse, the wife of a settler, and a former hospital orderly. Occasionally, Dr Balhetchet made his way from Singapore in an ambulance to treat patients. For serious illnesses, patients had to be loaded onto the trucks to the nearest town, Kuala Pilah, or go further to Seremban.

Scores of people lost their lives in Bahau and were buried in a nearby cemetery. One casualty was Bishop Adrien, who had moved into the settlement as well. His death, however, wasn't the result of a mosquito bite. While farming his land, he hit his foot with a hoe and had to have his leg amputated in a Negeri Sembilan hospital. He didn't survive. The prime mover of Bahau was dead at the age of 62, just a year after moving in.

Although they were surrounded by death and disease, one saving grace was that the Japanese left the settlers to their own devices—until towards the end of the Occupation. They were particular, however, on night patrols of the perimeter to keep out visitors. The Bogaars boys were rostered for patrol duty as well, armed with sticks and machetes. They were told to beat an old oil drum if there was a problem. There never was.

Then came one instruction: to grow cotton. It proved a non-starter given the arid ground and was soon abandoned. The second instruction had a greater impact. The Japanese called for labour corvees to help clear a rubber estate for what seemed to be an airstrip. The two brothers were rostered for this at least four times, for five days each time over a few months. Along with 40 or so ablebodied settlers, they were loaded onto trucks and dislodged at Ladang Geddes, where they joined a crowd of coolies, mainly local rubber tappers, both male and female, to remove stones and other debris.

That project too was abandoned after some months. Clearly, the Japanese were distracted. The Allies had stepped up attacks on the peninsula and seemed on the verge of winning the war. With the worst in mind, some Japanese soldiers appeared at the settlement one night to take away Eurasians whom they thought would be security risks if they continued living in Bahau. Bundled into lorries, they were interned at the Sime Road camp back in Singapore. Ironically, life as internees was better than in Bahau, they said after the war. They had better food and were liberated earlier than their Bahau counterparts.

For those still in the settlement, fear was mingled with hope. GEB recalled the excitement when coloured leaflets rained down from the sky, telling the residents to keep their spirits up. The British were returning. There was much weeping and shouting as the settlers rushed to catch the papers floating in the wind. Later, word came that they had to make four or five big bonfires which could be seen from the air. A couple of British soldiers parachuted into the settlement. Soon, big canisters of canned food and bread were dropped on them too.

On 15 August 1945, the Japanese surrendered.

Liberation

In Bahau, the day was remembered as the day the guerrillas emerged from the jungle. About a dozen armed Chinese men swarmed the settlement. They commandeered the settlement's van and were intent on taking over the running of the settlement. Among them was Lim, with a pistol at his side. Their high-handed attitude didn't endear them to the settlers and several rowdy rounds of negotiations were held as they insisted on taking over operations. All that changed when more British soldiers were parachuted into the settlement. In a week, the guerrillas melted away as suddenly as they had come. GEB, who had Lim's name and address, said he wrote to him after the war but there was no reply.

In their two months in Bahau, the British got to work setting up a communications network, tending to the sick and organising the food distribution, including army rations. There was much dancing and a few social events. A radio set blared Bing Crosby songs.

The settlers were getting ready for home and discarding whatever that was not needed. "We were slaughtering all our poultry and eating them. We brought some back to Singapore. But it must have been half the size of our flock," GEB recalled.

A group of teenagers brought his mother two pigs which they wanted her to cook for them. "We had a hell of a time trying to kill the pig, hanging it up by its legs and then stabbing away at its neck and all that. And my father was getting more and more furious with us. Because the pig was screaming and crying and howling." Slaughtering and cooking over, George found himself eating cooked pig's blood for the first time.

GEB Senior left for Singapore first. He returned later with a bus to collect the rest of his family and their belongings. They included the "wretched" earthenware pot which weighed down the bus and slowed their journey home, said GEB. The fields that they had so painstakingly cultivated were left fallow. Over time, the jungle took over the settlement.

III

Following in Dad's Footsteps

The Bogaarses returned to a Singapore they could hardly recognise: broken water pipes, no electricity, sky-high prices for food. Unemployment and lawlessness prevailed. Gambling and prostitution, legalised by the Japanese, were rife. The surrender of the Japanese didn't lead to a golden age for residents. In fact, the next two decades were just as tumultuous as various factions and political groups tussled violently for power. Singapore's founding prime minister, Lee Kuan Yew, recalled in his memoirs, *The Singapore Story*:

> The Japanese Occupation nightmare was over and people thought the good times were about to return. By early 1946, however, people realized that there was to be no return to the old peaceful, stable, free-and-easy Singapore. The city was packed with troops in uniform. They filled the newly opened cafés, bars and cabarets…. It was a world in turmoil where the hucksters flourished…. Much of the day-to-day business was still done on the black—now the free—market.

The British Military Administration (BMA) set up its secretariat at Empress Place, taking over from the civilian authorities. It was a period of confusion and uncertainty. The British had arrived to put things in order only three weeks after the surrender, during which chaos reigned. Even as the BMA set about rounding up war criminals, it had its share of corrupt officials who helped the collaborators and profiteers of the Japanese Occupation to continue to prosper. As a result of the inefficiency and mismanagement of the rice distribution, the BMA was cynically known as the "Black Market Administration".

However, by April 1946, when military rule ended, the BMA had managed to restore gas, water and electric services to above their pre-war capacity. The port was returned to civilian control, and seven private industrial, transportation and mining companies were given priority in importing badly needed supplies and materials. Japanese prisoners were used to repair docks and airfields.

The schools were reopened in March 1946, with 62,000 children enrolled. By the end of the year, Raffles College and the King Edward Medical College had both reopened as well.

In 1948, the Federation of Malaya was established as a move toward self-rule while Singapore continued as a separate Crown Colony under Governor Franklin Gimson. In that same year, however, the Malayan Communist Party launched an insurrection in Malaya and Singapore, and the British declared a State of Emergency that was to continue until 1960.

On returning to Singapore, the Bogaarses moved back into the Chancery Lane house, which had been kept very clean by the former Japanese occupants. It was also in a "very safe area" away from the turmoil that roiled urban centres teeming with opium addicts, revolutionaries and gangsters. GEB Senior was also recalled almost immediately to work. He was promoted to a higher pay scale and was awarded the Order of the British Empire for his loyalty. Soon, he was back in the Singapore Recreation Club as club secretary and taking part in his cricket matches.

As was his wont, GEB Senior didn't suffer the boys to laze around. The brothers were told to find themselves an education. They realised that the Christian brothers who were back from Bahau were conducting special classes. George studied with them—"mainly maps and English literature"—before the school year started in 1946. Then the 19 year old joined a class at St Joseph's Institution for what was his final year before obtaining the Higher School Certificate.

The class was a small group of young people who would be known today as overaged students: 17 to 20 year olds who had suffered the deprivations of war. Often these students were being taught by teachers not much older than them. Then he enrolled in Raffles College, which later merged with the King Edward VII College of Medicine to form the University of Malaya.

The post-war period wasn't a life of only books and study for the Bogaarses. When school was out, GEB Senior got his sons jobs at the Tanjong Pagar port. They were to be "assistant traffic controllers", not of ships, but of that most precious of commodities: rice. They had to supervise the loading and unloading, storage and storekeeping as well as prevent the looting and theft of rice from the Telok Blangah godowns. "There used to be shoot-outs between the police and these people. They were armed and they used to fight, shoot the police and there could have been a few deaths and injuries."

The Singapore Harbour Board, now the Port of Singapore Authority (PSA), was obliged to form its own police force. "There were many occasions when I had to stop labourers pilfering. And, you know, had to be very strict with the chaps. So that kind of thing went on for a year … until the Harbour Board finally got control of the situation."

Further education

In hindsight, GEB would thank the Japanese for his education. If there had been no war, which interrupted his education, he would have begged out of going to university and found some kind of employment. Instead, he had spent his two years in Bahau reading books from the extensive library that the Christian brothers had set up.

It was during his university days that GEB first came into contact with Singapore's future political leaders. He had volunteered to help conduct a social survey assessing the people's needs based on the 1947 census. In charge of the survey was Goh Keng Swee, then a colonial service officer in the Social Welfare Department.

One outcome of the study was the start of so-called soup kitchens, or People's Restaurants. *Goh Keng Swee: A Public Career Remembered*, a book published in 2011, reported GEB saying:

> Several of us students were involved in helping out in those kitchens, doing mostly administrative work such as recording the number of lunches given out, compiling inventories or preparing schedules and the like.
>
> I remember I was involved in a kitchen which was operating near [the old] Parliament House. Members of the public could go along and get lunch at a very low cost—I think it was about 30 or 35 cents in those days, for a meal of rice, vegetables and a little bit of meat.
>
> Later on, as the economy improved, more meals were offered at different prices—still around cost price—to cater to customers who wanted and could afford to pay for bigger portions of food.

It was also probably GEB's first introduction to the hierarchical system of the Civil Service. The Social Welfare Department was neither well-staffed nor did it have the best people. The officers were viewed, as he described in the book, as "the poorer cousins of the Administrative Service".

GEB received his bachelor's degree in 1950. In 1952, he was one of only two people to graduate with a master's degree from the merged University of Malaya. His master's thesis was on the history of the Tanjong Pagar Dock Company, the nucleus of Keppel Shipyard which he was later to be associated with.

Kennedy Gordon Tregonning, who was a lecturer at the University of Malaya's Department of History, recalled in his oral history interview that he tried offering GEB a job at the university. "He had done a very good piece of research on the Tanjong Pagar dock." The Head of the History Department Professor C. N. Parkinson, later famed for Parkinson's Law which posited that work expands to fill time allotted to it, wanted him employed as a graduate assistant. He told GEB he would support his efforts to get a scholarship to study for a doctorate abroad.

In what was probably his last interview in October 1991, published in the *Calibre* magazine, GEB said:

> The plan was for me to do my master's degree and then to do a higher degree at the London School of Oriental and African Studies and then return as an "academic" to the University of Malaya.
>
> I was all for this idea but my father thought otherwise. He said that teaching was a waste of time. He wanted me to join the Civil Service which he thought was a more worthwhile profession.
>
> Like a good son, I did. This was in 1952.

The rookie civil servant

GEB joined the Civil Service in 1952 when the institution was in chaos. The organisational structures and priorities were changed continually to fit the circumstances and the demands of local politicians and civil servants for rapid "Malayanisation", that is, the replacement of British expatriates with local-born residents.

This movement was a direct consequence of the war, which had jolted the thinking of the locals in a fundamental way: They realised that the British weren't invincible or infallible and that the locals needed to take their fate into their own hands. These were the first stirrings of nationalism and insistence on equal treatment for British and non-British subjects. Anti-colonialism, infused with leftist rhetoric, was on the rise. In the 1950s, salaries and staffing of the Civil Service became a bone of contention as local politicians tried to wrest control of the government machinery from the British.

The colonial service, which employed both locals and expatriates, was rivened by the same tensions. GEB Senior had found himself given the short end of the stick when civil servants were told that British expatriates would be given full back pay for three years of the Occupation as if they had been working, but not the locals. The local residents fought back and finally got partial restitution. Pay differences notwithstanding, GEB Senior never lost his allegiance to the British masters. GEB said in his oral recordings:

> He wouldn't have believed if you said that, "You know, this was the end of the British Empire and that this was a very severe blow to the prestige of the British." All the kinds of things that today are said about the effects of the Japanese Occupation of Singapore. He would not have believed it.

GEB recalled how at one dinner at home, a British defence official complained that some soldiers were not standing to attention when the British anthem was being played.

> I chipped in saying that I thought that maybe these people had been disillusioned and maybe they may have been justified in what they did. And my father turned around very sharply and really reprimanded me. He was most annoyed … telling me I was stupid and wrong and all to say these things. So he was that kind of a man.

GEB was one of 31 locals recruited into Division II, and the only local to be posted to the Commerce and Industry Department. He handled the barter trade between Singapore and the Riau Islands of

Indonesia, an activity that would take on a security dimension in later years. That was also when he met Lim Soo Peng, a third-generation rubber trader, with whom he formed a life-long friendship.

It is unclear when GEB moved to Division I but his rise was definitely rapid. He was promoted to Superscale G in 1960 and moved to E the following year. Looking back at his own storied career in later years, with postings to defence, foreign affairs and internal security, GEB would joke that it was a Civil Service habit to place its employees in areas that weren't relevant to what they had learnt in school.

The Malayanisation process was excruciatingly slow, hobbled by sticky questions, such as the number of locals competent enough to fill top jobs and the amount of recompense for expatriates who would suddenly be put out of work. According to a *Straits Times* report, in 1949, there were 119 locals out of 454 Division I officers. Five years later, in the beginning of 1954, there were 268 locals out of 671 Division I officers. The newspaper said that these "impressive figures did not tell the full story" as there was little change in the staffing ratios of the pinnacle Administrative Service. In his 1973 essay published in *Towards Tomorrow*, GEB, then Head of the Civil Service, elaborated on the numbers:

> Recruitment into the Singapore Administrative Service ... was pitifully small. In 1951, three appointments were made; in 1952, only one; in 1953 another three and in 1954 and 1955, four and six were appointed respectively. In 1956, when a measure of internal self-government was conferred on Singapore, the total number of local officers in Division I of the administrative branch of the Civil Service was 38 officers.

In 1952, Goh Keng Swee and his Civil Service colleague Kevin M. Byrne, together with journalist S. Rajaratnam and lawyer Lee Kuan Yew, formed the Council of Joint Action, to call for fairer terms of service for local civil servants, especially those with lower wages.

GEB was the treasurer of an informal group who called themselves the Singapore Administrative Officers Association which, together with 21 other unions and associations, was also part of the council.

Along with a few colleagues, GEB also formed a study group within the Administrative Service to thrash out what the response of civil servants should be if they were drawn into political conflict. It was disbanded after a while.

Neutrality or nationalism?

After 1955, as a result of the Rendel Constitution, Singapore was converted from a Crown Colony run by the British to a ministerial form of government run by local residents after the Legislative Assembly elections. The local ministers, while numerically superior, had, in truth, limited power, and civil servants were confronted with the question of whether to obey these new brooms or to go with the old ones.

David Marshall's oral history recording offers a look at how the Civil Service gave him short shrift, sticking him in a small cubbyhole under the main staircase at the old Parliament House. Infuriated, Marshall wrote his memos and minutes in red ink. This irked Governor John F. Nicoll so much that he told Marshall: "The Civil Service uses blue ink, the Auditor, green ink, and only I use red ink."

GEB became second deputy secretary at what was known then as the Treasury, the predecessor of the Ministry of Finance. His colonial boss when he first started was T. M. Hart. The first assistant financial secretary was Oon Khye Kiang while the third was Lim Chong Yah, the former head of the National Wages Council. In his autobiography, Lim referred to the class divisions in the colonial service. GEB was given an office of his own even though he was Oon's junior. "The British tended to treat their own kind as first-class citizens, Eurasians second class, while all other locals were considered third-class citizens," he wrote.

When the Labour Front under the leadership of David Marshall formed a coalition government after the 1955 Legislative Assembly elections, it made Malayanisation a top priority, pledging that the Singapore Civil Service would be localised in four years. His successor, Lim Yew Hock, who stepped into power just a year later, promised to carry on the work.

A new breed of civil servants known as supernumeraries was proposed. They were local-born civil servants who had been picked for specific senior appointments. They would be shadowing their British superiors until it was time for the British to pack up and leave. Today, they would be described as trainees or apprentices shadowing bosses, readying themselves to take over the post at a stipulated time.

But even as locals started filling top jobs, serving officers realised they had to answer not just to their colonial masters but also to the new political leaders who were taking control of the legislature and other political organisations. These local senior civil servants were finding themselves in direct conflict with the local politicians since, as civil servants, they were implementing the policy of their masters at Whitehall, who still controlled the key areas of civil service, treasury, internal defence, external affairs and legislation.

GEB recalled that there were many resignations which created a vacuum in the middle to senior ranks. The flip side was that it created room for the men who were to be credited for pioneering Singapore's development—Hon Sui Sen (1939–1965, with an interruption between 1942 and 1945 due to the war), Howe Yoon Chong (1949–1979), Sim Kee Boon (1953–1984), Ngiam Tong Dow (1959–1999) and J. Y. Pillay (1961–1995), among others.

Mayor's minions

One personality who grated on the nerves of the Civil Service, especially the expatriates, was Ong Eng Guan, who was elected in the mayoral elections to the City Council in December 1957. He enjoyed flaunting his connection with the masses, pursued popular policies like lowering licence fees for hawkers, taxi-drivers and trishaw riders, and made sure civil servants knew who the boss was by ordering them round and dressing them down in public. He had no qualms ordering the staff out of their offices to sweep the roads in the city. There was even a roster.

For all his bullying and berating, however, Ong brought in results. He attacked corruption, made sure that civil servants responded promptly to complaints and provided vital services such as standpipes, street lighting, creches and public clinics.

GEB recalled:

> There were a lot of entrenched interests in the City Council in those days before Ong Eng Guan took over. The public was treated abominably, and he gave the place a shaking up. It was a frightening sight to see. At the same time, lots of us were quite happy that this had taken place. We had had our personal experiences with the City Council which were, by and large, very unpleasant. Whilst we were horrified to see how he did it, at the same time we were quite pleased that he did it.

His fellow civil servants at that time, Ngiam Tong Dow and Sim Kee Boon, acknowledged that Ong's action jolted the bureaucracy out of its malaise and contributed to the image of the PAP as a party which could get things done.

Settling into self-government

It was the PAP's turn in government after winning 43 out of 51 seats in the May 1959 general election. It inherited nine ministries and a 28,000-strong Civil Service that was no longer dominated by expatriates. GEB said in his oral recordings:

> It was a tremendous surprise that they had succeeded in capturing so many seats. From the early days of my youth, I have lived through the situation where the City Council, or Municipal Council as it was then, was always in the hands of the British, or in the hands of those who listened to the British anyhow, and did what they were told. Overnight, the whole thing changed. Then it was clear to absolutely everyone that the PAP would now be a party to be reckoned with.

Lee Kuan Yew became the Prime Minister, a position he retained till November 1990. Goh Keng Swee became the Minister for Finance and picked Hon Sui Sen as his Permanent Secretary. GEB remained as Deputy Secretary. In 1970, Hon Sui Sen became the Minister for Finance till his death in 1983. He was to be the man GEB relied on for support throughout his career.

When the PAP took office in 1959, the number of local officers in Division I of the Civil Service was about 575, and of these, there were 59 officers in the Administrative Service, seven holding the key appointments of Permanent Secretary in the various ministries. Commenting on those days in the 1973 essay he penned for *Towards Tomorrow*, GEB wrote:

> It would have been one of the easiest things for the Government to have gone along with the general mood and fashion of the day—a mood and fashion which had started in the newly independent countries of Asia after the Second World War—to denigrate and abuse the Civil Service until by gradual exhaustion it loses all confidence in itself as well as the respect of the public for which it is paid to serve. The results of such attrition are a collapse of the Administration and its floundering inefficiency, corruption and graft.

Goh Keng Swee entered the Finance Ministry only to find that the last government had dipped into the reserves and used up $200 million. He foresaw a budget deficit of more than $14 million for 1959. To avoid putting the PAP's first year of government in the red, austerity measures were announced, including pay cuts for civil servants and a freeze on all new appointments. The ministers would lead by example, paring down their pay from $2,650 a month to $2,050. The prime minister slashed his from $3,650 to $3,050. A saving of some $10 million was made at once. Increased taxation was then introduced which resulted in some $20 million more for the national coffers.

In his book, *The Singapore Story*, Lee Kuan Yew maintained that the pay cuts were "significant but not devastating", affecting 6,000 of the 14,000 civil servants. They stood to lose their variable allowances but only ten per cent would suffer cuts of more than $250 a month while the most senior would be hit with a $400 cut.

This did not allay the fears of the largely English-educated Civil Service, who had worried about how they would be treated by a PAP government with its prominent Chinese base. Depending on salary, the pay cuts could come up to a substantial proportion. In an interview with John Drysdale, who wrote *Singapore: Struggle for Success*, GEB said:

> There was a lot of privation that we had to go through. We had servants who had to go. Lots of commitments came to an end, car loans, house loans. I could see it was not being done merely because they wanted to have a whack at the Civil Service. It was because they felt this was good for the Civil Service and for the general good of the country.
>
> The Prime Minister personally paid visits to departments, ripped them open and turned them upside down … Civil servants were terrified; they would quote a phrase to each other, thought to have emanated from the Prime Minister—"We should get down on our bended knees and thank God that nothing worse than the pay cuts that had taken place."

GEB was referring to a speech made by Lee to the Legislative Assembly on 21 July 1959:

> I say to the Civil Service and their present rather inept leaders who have begun what they believe to be a revolutionary movement against the Government, that if nothing else more catastrophic happens to them than the loss of allowances in the top brackets of the Civil Service, and the fact that they have to face fiercer competition from the non-English-educated members of the service, then they should go down on their bended knees and thank the gods that their souls have been spared.

The reaction of the Civil Service to the pay cuts was visceral. The wheel had come full circle for the PAP. Just as the British had been confronted by the Council of Joint Action after it was created by Goh, Byrne and Rajaratnam in September 1952, with external assistance from Lee to "put vigour into Malayanisation and to score political points off the government", the PAP was now faced with a similarly named body seeking to overturn its decisions. But there was a key difference: the civil servants were facing elected politicians who had docked their own pay, which knocked out the argument about political self-aggrandisement. The politicians were leading by example. "Unlike my previous masters, both local and colonial, self-interest meant nothing to the new leaders," GEB said.

In his memoirs, Lee Kuan Yew said he was exasperated by the reaction of civil servants who did not appreciate the graver challenges posed by the communists, who were getting more aggressive with their United Front strategy. The pay cuts were to show the Chinese-educated majority that the English-educated were prepared to make sacrifices for the public good. "Some of the senior officers had to give up their maids—too bad, but the country was facing greater hardships and perils, and we had to convince people that this government would govern in the interests of all."

To keep the civil servants abreast of the vision of the PAP government, Lee decided that they needed to be re-oriented. On 15 August 1959, he established the Political Study Centre and told civil servants at the inauguration:

> This Civil Service Study Centre is, in part, an attempt to telescope into a study course the main elements of the political and social forces which caused the post-war revolutions in Asia. If nothing else, you will at least understand what was the genesis of the forces that have shaken the British raj under which nearly all of you were recruited, and under which you were guaranteed a lifetime of service with a pension at the end.
>
> Some of you may be bewildered and perplexed by what you may consider the impatience with which we are asking for things to be done. If so, then I hope that at the end of your course in this Study Centre, if you do not sympathise with our impatience, you will at least understand it. You will at least appreciate why we consider it so vital for the democratic machinery to be in tune with the temper of the people and tempo of political change if the democratic state is to survive.
>
> Whether an administration functions efficiently and smoothly in the interests of the people as a whole or in the interests of a small section of the people, depends upon the policies of the Ministers. But it is your responsibility to make sure that there is an efficient Civil Service.

GEB was to recall this speech when he himself addressed civil servants undergoing orientation in 1973.

> During these five years before entry into Malaysia, the Civil Service had learnt what the Prime Minister meant when he said that it was vital for the democratic machinery to be in tune with the temper of the people and tempo of political change if the democratic state was to survive.
>
> The Civil Service had seen the many forms and guises constitutional challenges to the basis of democracy could take. It had learnt that sensitive and spontaneous responses were vital if the issues confronting the Government had to be met and resolved.

A key challenge was changing the ethos of the Civil Service, from regarding the people as aliens to treating them as citizens. Laws had to be changed and institutions re-organised to deal with the people's social and economic needs. One big step, for example, was the establishment of the Housing & Development Board to rectify the housing shortage. But the bigger test was how the Civil Service would respond to the Communist United Front which had "opened up every single possible political issue from that on education and culture to labour and economic development in successive waves of agitation in attempts to unseat and topple the Government," wrote GEB in *Towards Tomorrow*.

By 1961, two years after the PAP took office, GEB had moved up at least three rungs to Administrative Service Superscale Grade E. He would have been hit hard by the pay cuts of 1959, which included the removal of cost of living allowances payable to mid-level and senior civil servants two years earlier. This was despite his being part of the implementation process as he was the secretary of the Cabinet Budget Committee on Expenditure, which decided on the size of the cuts. It was not until 1961 that allowances were restored and later still, in 1973, that salary increases were implemented.

Historian John Drsydale said GEB's position gave him an inside view, not only of the effects that the government's policies were having on the Civil Service, but also of the men behind the policy. GEB concurred: "I got to know their thinking very quickly and could see what was happening politically."

Political education came soon. Despite self-government, former mayor Ong Eng Guan, now appointed National Development Minister, was behaving like the martinet that he had been in the City Council.

A powerful Hokkien orator with a substantial Chinese following, he was said to be running neck-to-neck with Lee Kuan Yew to be prime minister and spent much time seeking to pack the PAP's rank-and-file with his own cronies. GEB recalled:

> Very few civil servants were aware that the PAP was divided into factions. A group of people who used expressions like "Comrade" seemed united, one in thought. But things began to crack when Ong Eng Guan became Minister for National Development, taking the law into his own hands.
>
> When I saw the brakes being applied by Goh Keng Swee, the Minister for Finance, I realised things were not so straightforward. It looked as if this fellow wanted to carve a more important position for himself than he had. There were others who were determined to see that he didn't.

Those brakes were applied when Dr Goh showed GEB a scrap of paper on which Ong had scribbled a request for $400 million towards what he described as "his housing". Bogaars was instructed to "turn the thing down".

It was one of several such requests that had come to the Cabinet's attention. Fractious party meetings were held to put Ong in his place. His PAP comrades tried to get him suspended from the Legislative Assembly for dishonourable conduct. A committee of inquiry was set up to investigate his comments on nepotism. His ministerial colleagues started hiving off parts of the National Development Ministry to other ministries and agencies to handle. The public housing portfolio, the biggest project, was passed on to Lim Kim San.

Although his power play upset his party colleagues, Ong's popularity with the people did not wane. After he was expelled from the PAP, he contested as an independent in the constituency of Hong Lim in the 1961 by-election. He beat PAP's Jek Yuen Thong handsomely, with 73.31 per cent of the votes. He later formed the United People's Party with himself as secretary-general.

The shenanigans of one maverick were nothing compared to the fratricidal warfare waged within the PAP, which had Lim Chin Siong heading the pro-communist faction. Although the Malayan

Communist Party had been outlawed and active members detained during the many sweeps in the 12-year Emergency which ended in 1960, it coped by changing its tactics. It started instigating lawlessness in communities such as the Chinese-educated students and trade unionists while also pursuing the constitutional path.

Lim was incarcerated after the 1956 Chinese middle school riots and released when the PAP took power in 1959. He was placed in Goh Keng Swee's Finance Ministry as a political secretary. Wary of Lim's influence, Dr Goh told GEB to keep him "busy". Except that Lim was never in the office long enough for any work assignment, GEB recalled.

At this point in his career, GEB had already worked for the colonial government, the David Marshall and Lim Yew Hock governments, and experienced a multitude of demonstrations and riots that involved pro-communists such as the Anti-National Service Riots in 1954 and the Hock Lee bus riots in 1955. From now on he would be serving the PAP government.

IV

Nearly Not Married

Who would have thought that a young civil servant and a middle-aged tobacco tycoon would be vying for the same woman? And that the scandal would make the news?

George Edwin Bogaars did something exceptional for a Eurasian in those days. He fell in love with a Chinese woman, a mother of two children. He was then 27, Director of Commerce and Trade in the colonial service. He met 23-year-old Dorothy Lee Kian Neo at a party which was intended by relatives to matchmake GEB with a girl from the Klasse family. The year was 1954.

Described in the media as a "colony beauty", Dorothy had been customarily married to a millionaire more than twice her age. Wee Thiam Soo was a tobacco magnate and proprietor of the Seventh Storey Hotel.

Notice of the Bogaars-Lee marriage had been up at the Supreme Court Registry of Civil Marriages for weeks. The notice described Lee as "divorced by Chinese custom" but Wee evidently disagreed. Wee lodged a caveat to stop the wedding, insisting that Dorothy was still his legal wife.

Registrar for marriages A. M. Spryut was flummoxed. He had never had to face such a situation. The Civil Marriage Ordinance of the time, however, did empower him to decide on the next course of action—to marry or not to marry the couple. He didn't have to decide. Lawyers for Lee and Wee negotiated a deal and the caveat was withdrawn in early October. GEB was away in Ottawa, Canada, attending a conference during this time.

There was opposition from GEB's side of the family as well. In those early days, Eurasians tended to marry each other. Dorothy was not considered good enough to belong to the Eurasian upper crust. GEB Senior, for example, played an active role in the Singapore Recreation Club, as a committee member and a cricketer. His wife, Edwina, belonged to the illustrious Tessensohn family. Her grandfather Edwin was the first Eurasian legislative councillor in the Straits Settlements in 1923. Both were leading Eurasian families.

GEB's daughter Christina, a writer living in the United States, said that there was some friction with relatives who thought her father had married down. Dorothy was considered an outsider. She did not have any family connections to speak of. She was an orphan, non-Christian and grew up independent-minded and strong-willed. She was the very antithesis of GEB's own mother, a traditional housewife from an established Eurasian family.

Christina said that there was also a perception that her mother was a gold-digger, even though she had forsaken her life of luxury to marry GEB. "She had ball gowns, jewellery, servants, cooks, drivers, houses built in her name, etc. I think everything you would want from a Cinderella story. *But* she left all that for Dad—at that time a lowly civil servant making very little money," she told the author in an e-mail interview. In fact, she added, it was her mother who bought the house where the family lived later, at Ewe Boon Road in Bukit Timah. She bought it "for a steal" because the house was coffin-shaped and was number 4, a number traditionally associated with bad luck. It was originally two separate buildings linked by a walkway. Then a sitting room was built to link both units.

The wedding took place on 27 November 1954 at the Catholic Sacred Heart Church in Tank Road. GEB's younger brother, Brian, was his best man while Dorothy was led up the aisle by a Mr A. Jansen, according to newspaper reports. Their first child, Paulina, was born in 1957. Christina came next in 1964, followed by George Michael two years later. Evidently, GEB had decided to stick to the family tradition of naming at least one male in the family George. George Michael has continued the tradition, naming one of his two sons George Matthew.

Dorothy had converted to Catholicism to marry GEB. She became a devout Catholic. She started a jumble sale once a month at St Bernadette's Church in Zion Road. Over the years, this morphed into the St Vincent de Paul Thrift Shop.

Home life

From his children's recollections, they had a happy home life. Never mind that the bungalow was airy with eaves that encouraged visitors like snakes. And because the Bukit Timah canal had yet to be built, the area was prone to flooding. For the children, it was a great space to grow up. GEB had built an aviary in the garden for finches and quails and kept two tanks of fish. Visitors were always coming and going and Christmases were big affairs with Dorothy cooking up a storm. Sundays were spent picnicking in Katong Park; holidays were drives to Kuantan or Cameron Highlands in Malaysia.

GEB was always busy with work, whether at home or in the office, but he seemed nothing like his own father in the way he interacted with his children. They remembered a carefree, open-minded and big-hearted father, who loved driving fancy cars, courtesy of a friend who collected and refurbished them. His son Michael, a retired senior lieutenant-colonel of the Republic of Singapore Air Force, recalled:

> I'm not talking about exotic cars or supercars, but convertibles and grand tourers. I recall he had an MGB with a rag top, a Sunbeam Rapier and a Lancia Fulvia. He would spend time on the weekends washing them and tending to them, maybe even servicing them. This was the era when car owners did things like timing adjustments and gapping the spark plugs themselves. He loved to take drives in his cars with the top down and I would go with him sometimes.

One early morning in September 1971, the family had four visitors who turned up uninvited. Four men, clad only in swimming trunks with their faces masked by handkerchiefs, stole into the house and held up the family. They were armed with parangs. Paulina, then 14 years old, said they went up to her parents' bedroom and cut the phone line, which was an extension line.

> Dad said later that because he did not have his glasses on, he could not identify them. Mum pleaded with them not to disturb the two young sleeping children and they did not. They came into my bedroom with Dad and tried to look for valuables. I remember Dad sitting at the end of my bed with his hand on my leg telling me not to worry. I thought they were searching for snakes!
>
> As they left with Mum's jewellery, cash and some bottles of alcohol, Dad used the phone in the sitting room to call the Police. They came very quickly but only recovered the alcohol, which had been thrown into the bushes. The burglars were never caught, as far as I know.

The robbers got away with $5,000 in cash and jewellery. Up till today, both daughters still wonder at the timing of the burglary. Their mother had taken out the jewellery she kept in a bank safe deposit to wear to a dinner just that night with GEB. The house was also well-hidden in a cul-de-sac. As Christina said: "In fact there were several big bungalows on that road, but the robbers chose our small house? None of the other homes were burgled as far as I know. I often wondered if it was targeted at Dad and intended as a 'message'?"

Unlike his own father, GEB didn't put his children's nose to the grindstone and immerse them in their studies or future career paths, although he was still watchful over their grades. "I think he still smarted from being told what to do by his own dad, and so he didn't push us into government like his dad did to him," said Christina. That did not mean his children were slouches in school. Both Christina and Paulina went overseas for their higher studies and Paulina has settled in Adelaide, Australia, while Christina is halfway across the globe in the United States.

"He gave me a book about the science of chicken rearing—his dad had threatened him with a caning if he let their chickens die, so he must have studied how to feed and raise them."

The civil servant known for being tight-fisted with money also surfaced in the father sometimes. Christina recalls how he had helped her bake curry puffs for her secondary school fair. She had not figured out how to price each puff and lost money. "He was not impressed with me when he was forced to make up the difference." He knew the school principal well and stood there grumbling about it to her. He also gave Christina "a long lecture about profit and loss."

Christina said that people flocked to her father because he was so well-read and an entertaining conversationalist.

> He was very comfortable being the centre of attention. He did not actively seek the limelight. He really had a certain charisma that you had to experience in person. Photos and videos don't do him justice. When he listened and paid attention to you, you felt like you really mattered.

Tan Siok Sun, who worked with him in the Foreign Ministry, would agree. She said he wasn't someone who could be missed in a crowded room. It was more than just his height, which was about six feet, or his bearing: "a big, huggable teddy bear—he would just stand out as a person."

A parting of ways

GEB Senior and his wife Edwina migrated to Australia a little after the wedding in 1954, following in the footsteps of their daughter Patricia, who had settled with her husband in Melbourne a few years before. The couple had set up a centre for students, known as Malaya Hall, in Melbourne. With his parents and sister abroad, GEB was left in Singapore with his brother Brian, who rose through the police ranks and retired as Assistant Police Commissioner in July 1978. He died in December 2015. Both the Bogaars brothers were religious people, especially Brian, who was a deacon with the Church of St Ignatius.

GEB's marriage lasted till February 1977, when Dorothy was granted a divorce by the High Court on the grounds of cruelty. She received custody of their three children. GEB did not contest the suit. No one was keen to expand on the differences the couple had, but the marriage had clearly broken down. GEB had entangled himself with a younger woman. There was at least one public screaming match when Dorothy caught the pair together.

In a letter to his daughter Christina in his later years, he described the parting as "a tremendous weight off my conscience and my life". Christina would only describe her parents as a gorgeous couple who were terribly in love in the beginning, but their strong-willed personalities got in the way. GEB expected Dorothy to be a traditional housewife. She, on the other hand, valued her independence.

After the divorce, Christina said that Dorothy, Michael and she had moved to a flat on Lloyd Road so the children could be close to their schools. Twenty-year-old Paulina was already in Adelaide at university. "Dad moved to a flat in Shenton Way to be close to work.

Whenever I saw him, it was work, work and work. He just immersed himself in his work." For companionship, he kept a Pomeranian called Penhurst Campbell, who was also known as Prinsz.

Although Dorothy was given custody of the children, GEB would spend time on Sundays with them.

> He would pick me up and my brother from my mum's and take us to church and breakfast. We'd then go for a movie at the Cathay or laze around at his place. Sometimes we went for a swim at the Pyramid Club or the Lady Hill Hotel, where he would read the papers while we splashed around with our friends.
>
> It seemed like he was on the boards of many companies at that time. I remember he said that he "sat on the NZ Cheese board", and I asked if the toothpicks hurt. He had a good laugh at that one.

Post-divorce, GEB renewed his passion for collecting clocks, describing himself as a "horrorologist". Ex-colleagues remembered how the walls of his apartment at Marina House were plastered with some 30 clocks. Michael said it was a ritual for him to spend a few minutes each day winding, adjusting and playing with them. They made a fine din but would always be switched off when the children stayed over.

Christina added that he had the chiming clocks set to chime one after another so they could all enjoy the different sounds. Most of the clocks were set to chime from dawn to dusk and turned themselves back on in the morning. "He spent a lot of time explaining the different types of clocks—8-day, 12-day, mariner's, grandfather, grandmother, etc."

When GEB died, his collection of clocks was divided among Paulina, Christina, Michael and close friends. Paulina has an additional keepsake—a pen stand that was a gift from Lee Kuan Yew to her father.

When his two daughters were living in Adelaide, he kept up a constant correspondence with them, giving them fatherly advice and telling them what he was up to. In one letter to Paulina, he wrote of his irritation when a relative asked if he would remarry. He didn't want to nor did he need to, he said, as he had three beautiful children. "He still referred to my mum as 'his wife' when talking to people," said Christina.

The couple appeared to have mended their fences in later years, with Dorothy making a point of seeing GEB every Saturday in the last few years of his life. According to Christina:

> They still communicated through us and occasionally in person. Through the course of his physical decline which lasted nearly ten years, my mum would visit him in hospital and at his home. She felt close to him and I think they made their peace before he died. She helped me plan his wake and funeral. She was very distraught at the funeral.

Dorothy outlived GEB by almost 27 years, dying in February 2019.

V

On the Hunt
for Communists

Reports and records of Singapore's pre-merger days with Malaysia and the subsequent Separation are unsurprisingly focused on the politicians on both sides. Little has been said about the men who stood unobtrusively in the background, the silent witnesses who had to carry out the decisions of politicians. GEB was one such witness, entrusted with state secrets and privy to the big events as they unfolded.

He is mentioned intermittently in the memoirs of national icons like Lee Kuan Yew, referred to in books on Singapore's past and in the oral history records of pioneer civil servants. Such mentions do not shed more light on his role, but these glimpses are enough to demonstrate his stature and the amount of trust and faith that the PAP leadership had in him. For example, GEB was one of three civil servants privy to the details of the Separation document that was ironed out between Goh Keng Swee and Tun Abdul Razak in Kuala Lumpur on 6 August 1965, according to the former's biography, *Goh Keng Swee: A Portrait*. The other two civil servants in the loop were the Head of Civil Service, Stanley Stewart, and the Cabinet Secretary,

Wong Chooi Sen. Lee Kuan Yew's memoir, *The Singapore Story*, tells how, in those frantic days before Separation became official on 9 August, Lee had called in GEB: "to be quite certain he was confident we could contain any threat from the communists in an independent Singapore as long as we did not allow them to rebuild their organisation. He assured me that we could."

Lee had consulted GEB because he was then Head of the Special Branch, although what he actually did during his four-year term before Independence is still very much under wraps. He may be considered Singapore's spymaster at the most tumultuous period in Singapore's history, as the country made its tortuous way from British colony, through limited self-governance, a Malaysian state and finally, to a new nation fraught with communist and communal tensions.

The tall, big, bespectacled man didn't look like the stereotype of the spy engaged in cloak-and-dagger operations. In fact, he wasn't even a trained policeman, being a deputy secretary at the Treasury.

Eric John Linsell had just been made head of the Special Branch in 1959 when Khaw Kai Boh, the specially groomed local Acting Director, resigned in April. Linsell was an experienced police officer and, under the provisions of retirement for colonial officers, was due to leave the service in 1961. Lee Kuan Yew did not think much of the man. "He did not strike me as having that subtlety of mind necessary to understand communist tactics and strategy," he said in his memoir. He was more impressed by Linsell's subordinates Richard Byrne Corridon and Ahmad Khan, both expatriates who had been active operatives from the late 1940s, with their "shrewd and perceptive analysis of information on the communists".

Corridon had played an instrumental part in the communist round-ups in the mid-1950s, when Lim Yew Hock had invoked the Preservation of Public Security Ordinance (PPSO). In an interview with historian John Drysdale, Corridon said that British intelligence had been keeping an eye on Lee Kuan Yew and Goh Keng Swee while they were studying in the United Kingdom because of their speeches against the empire and their contacts with British communists. The British feared that they were closet communists who would fire up the communist underground in Singapore on their return. The Special Branch chief at that time, Alan Blades, wondered if the two should be detained on arrival and interned on St John's Island. But Corridon, who had his own sources in England, advised that they be left alone: "Let's see how they shape up."

Khan came to Singapore from the Punjab in 1934 at the age of 22 and joined the Singapore Police Force. He was well known as a superb investigator, rising through the ranks and retiring as a Superintendent of Police. He was chiefly responsible for the destruction of the Malayan Communist Party (MCP) Indian section. He returned to Pakistan in 1964.

Lee was unhappy that the Special Branch was made up more of policemen-types than security analysts. He wanted the Special Branch to be more like the British MI5. To re-orientate the agency, Lee asked a British intelligence and security officer, Christopher Herbert, to turn the Special Branch from a police outfit to an intelligence agency. GEB, then at the Treasury, became Herbert's liaison officer.

GEB said in a post-retirement interview with *The Straits Times* that it was Herbert who furnished the prime minister with the names of three civil servants who could head the reorganised Special Branch. "I was one of them," he said. "When it was clear the other two did not want the job, I knew that if I said no too, it would be very difficult to come up with other names."

Although GEB was to take over from Linsell in August, word of his appointment had already been leaked to the press as early as January 1961. *The Straits Times* reported that the Superscale Grade E

55

officer was being put in what is known as a supernumerary capacity, in preparation for the job as chief. Aware, perhaps, that there might be public concern that a non-policeman was getting the job, the formal press announcement on the appointment that came later made a point of saying that he had undergone "a special period of training in London".

There was no elaboration on the type of training. Presumably, this was at the MI5 Grosvenor Square headquarters in London. According to writer Leon Comber's *Malaya's Secret Police 1945–60*, selected Senior Special Branch officers of the colonies were sent for the Advanced Intelligence Course. Besides briefings on the end of the Malayan Emergency, they learnt about the "writing, processing and dissemination of information".

The Special Branch: Pre-Bogaars

In 1948, when the Malayan Emergency was declared, the Special Branch, precursor of the Internal Security Department, was set up by the British to root out subversive elements, such as communists and other threats to British sovereignty.

It was a much-feared outfit, given the scope of emergency regulations which included the imposition of the death penalty for those found in possession of arms, ammunition or explosives. The police had special powers of arrest and search, closure of buildings, requisition and seizure of properties.

At the same time, the Communist Party of Malaya (or Malayan Communist Party, as it was commonly called) was outlawed. In Singapore, activists in its proxy organisations, such as town committees and organisations of trade unions, as well as students were arrested over the next few years, leaving a substantial vacuum in the party hierarchy.

This State of Emergency was not to end until 31 July 1960, when Tunku Abdul Rahman, Prime Minister of the Malayan Federation, declared it over.

It was against this backdrop that Singapore's experiment with democracy took place. As outlined in the Rendel Constitution, Singapore was given limited self-government in 1955, allowing it to take charge of domestic affairs while defence and foreign affairs remained in the hands of the British. Other changes included the formation of a Legislative Assembly where 25 out of 32 representatives would be elected by the people. Emergency regulations were replaced by the Preservation of Public Security Ordinance (PPSO) providing for detention without trial.

David Marshall from the Labour Front became Singapore's first Chief Minister after his party secured ten seats, the biggest number among the parties which contested. He lasted only for slightly more than a year before he was replaced by Lim Yew Hock.

While the colonial army and Special Branch might have quelled the extreme militant tactics used by the Malayan Communist Party in the jungles of the peninsula by the mid-1950s, there was still the problem of urban unrest in the cities, especially in Singapore. The Communist United Front of disaffected workers and trade unionists, and students from the Chinese middle schools were intent on turning every policy into a national issue. Only about one-third of the 275 strikes called in 1955 were for better wages and working conditions; the remainder were sympathy strikes or strikes to protest imprisonment of labour union officials, according to *Men In White*, a book detailing the PAP's political history.

Although Marshall declined to set the police on them, his successor, Lim Yew Hock, had no such qualms. He reached for the PPSO often. Over the next four years, Lim cracked down hard on the pro-communist elements and anti-colonial activists. He de-registered organisations and started arresting agitators, which only served to rouse the ire of disaffected workers and students.

In the so-called October Revolution of 1956, which had striking students and workers out on the streets, 259 people were arrested under PPSO and another 1,000 detained for rioting, breaking the curfew and other offences, according to *Original Sin* author Kumar Ramakrishna. Included in the sweep were 14 pro-communist PAP members and trade unionists, such as Lim Chin Siong and Fong Swee Suan.

Internal security had been a bone of contention. The British wanted to have the final say on arrests under the PPSO. The initially proposed Internal Security Council (ISC) gave the British the casting vote in case of a deadlock. This issue was a thorn in Singapore's side and Marshall had staked his political career on getting it changed. He resigned when he couldn't make any headway with the British during constitutional talks.

The British changed their minds after witnessing Lim Yew Hock's tough action against the communists. Thus in 1959, the Rendel Constitution was replaced with the State of Singapore Constitution. The local government would be vested with full internal governing powers, while the British would continue to be responsible for Singapore's defence and foreign affairs. They agreed that internal security would be managed by an Internal Security Council comprising three representatives each from Britain and Singapore, with the casting vote to be held by the sole representative of the Federation of Malaya.

Lim's actions, however, didn't deal the death blow to the communists. While not renouncing armed struggle, they changed tactics and decided to pursue a parallel constitutional route to achieve their aims.

His heavy-handed approach, so welcomed by the British, had the opposite effect on the Chinese-speaking electorate. They made their disapproval plain in the 1959 elections by voting in what they viewed as the more leftist PAP, which had promised the release of detainees. The PAP captured just 53.4 per cent of the votes cast but, in the first-past-the-post electoral system, that amounted to 43 out of 51 seats in the Legislative Assembly.

The Special Branch: Under Bogaars

These were the tumultuous political circumstances which preceded GEB's appointment to the Special Branch. How GEB took to doing intelligence work after dealing with financial matters over the past nine years is mostly a blank. Interestingly, GEB recalled he had fewer problems interacting with the trained Special Branch officers than the politicians who had asked him to take over. They viewed him as a Treasury man without any real expertise or experience in security matters. "When it came to the crunch, I could always detect this feeling among the politicians—you know, what did I know about security matters anyway and all that," GEB said in an interview with *The Straits Times* in 1981.

GEB must have had the blessings of his minister, Goh Keng Swee, the close confidant of Lee Kuan Yew, who appointed GEB to the post. His focus was on making sure that the Special Branch operated as the "brains" of internal security, as Lee wanted, giving feedback and providing intelligence for decisions to be made by the politicians.

There could have been another consideration: Besides the pressing need for a local in the post, GEB was not Chinese. Race was an important consideration in those days, as minutes of the Internal Security Council testified. A lot of time was spent discussing the morale of police officers and the appointments of senior officers. In

1962, John Le Cain, another Eurasian, was appointed Commissioner of Police. Unlike GEB, however, he was a career policeman.

Lee Kuan Yew might have also considered how a former director of the Special Branch, Khaw Kai Boh, who served under the Lim Yew Hock government, had "changed sides". When the PAP took power in 1959, Khaw left to join the Malayan Chinese Association in Malaya and was subsequently appointed a senator and minister by the Malayan government. Lee would rail against him often during the 1964 general election, the first for the merged Malaysia. Thus, having a Special Branch director who understood the unique circumstances facing Singapore, the politics of the PAP and communist strategies, and who could be expected to sink roots in Singapore, would be of paramount importance to Lee.

Promises to keep

Although it had emerged triumphant after the 1959 polls, the PAP was also in a quandary. The PAP leaders had promised to release the detainees despite reservations about their pro-communist agenda. In the end only eight, including Lim Chin Siong, were released in the first instance. The rest were released over time. The PAP had also changed its mind about abolishing the Internal Security Council, one of the campaign promises it had made.

Fratricidal infighting characterised much of the PAP during this period. Left-wing members thought the leadership had veered from its original aims and tried to oust Lee from the party's Central Executive Committee. When Lee asked for a motion of confidence in the Legislative Assembly, 13 of his own party members abstained. He sacked them from the party and deprived those associated with them of their public offices. This was the start of the split in the PAP, which led to the formation of the Barisan Sosialis. Historian Lee Ting Hui estimated that the PAP lost 60 to 70 per cent of its membership then.

While the people watched the political theatrics taking place in the open, they did not know of fierce wrangling in the Internal Security Council, which was dithering over action against communists. Like the British, the PAP wanted the communists suppressed, but with as little damage to its own standing with the Chinese-speaking as possible. It wanted arrests made quickly also because of an ultimatum from Tunku Abdul Rahman, Prime Minister of the Federation, who had placed the elimination of the communist threat as a condition for Singapore's merger with Malaya. The British, however, were concerned about how the arrests would be viewed in London, especially if evidence against the communists was not compelling. It was also wary about being used by the PAP to eliminate its political opponents.

Plunged into the frenzied politics of that time, GEB started work even before his formal appointment. *The Straits Times* reported that he was among a team of plainclothes police officers involved in a raid on 18 June 1961, which led to the arrests of 11 people and the seizure of three hand grenades said to be for use in the assassination of the prime minister and his ministers.

The "assassination" plot, however, turned out to be a hoax perpetrated by a detective and a police informer. They had planted the grenades to fabricate evidence, a police statement released a few days later said.

It would appear that the informant and the CID detective embellished what may have been an attempt to create disorder at the rally into an assassination plot to ingratiate themselves with the police, the informer in the hope of a reward and the detective presumably hoping for a promotion.

A medical doctor and former detainee, Poh Soo Kai, in his book *Living in a Time of Deception*, said that the 34-year-old Bogaars "undoubtedly" called the shots on that raid. "He tarnished the start of the localisation of the Special Branch to say the least." Poh was arrested in February 1963, along with more than a hundred others in a security swoop codenamed Operation Coldstore. He was detained without trial under the Preservation of Public Security Ordinance and only released 17 years later in August 1982.

Declassified minutes of Internal Security Council monthly meetings showed that GEB started participating in them from August 1961 as an "advisor". There were three representatives from the British side, with the British High Commissioner from 1959–1963 Lord Selkirk as the Council chairman. On the Singapore side were Lee Kuan Yew, Goh Keng Swee and the Home Affairs Minister, Ong Pang Boon. The Federal representative was Ismail Abdul Rahman, Minister for Internal Security. Over the course of 1962, the Singapore side tried to make the case for arrests and detentions of those involved in a communist conspiracy, taking what academic Kumar Ramakrishna called a "maximalist view" of what would constitute a threat to the State.

While the British wanted hard evidence of an impending revolt or violence before making arrests, the Singapore side countered that even if the communists did not take violent action, there was still the threat that they could win the elections based on Chinese working class support. If this happened, Singapore would be in direct conflict with the Malay-dominated Federal government. Already, the Barisan Sosialis and the pro-communist camp were against the terms of merger that the PAP had worked out with the Tunku's government, arguing that they did not give Singapore parity with the other Malaysian states. They had tried to derail the referendum on the merger held in September 1962, but did not succeed in getting the electorate to cast blank votes. Among other things, the PAP government had pointed out that casting a blank vote meant a vote in favour of its own proposal.

In the end, the PAP's merger proposal giving Singapore autonomy in labour, education and other agreed matters collected 70 per cent of the vote. Still, there was no indication that the opposing forces would stand down. They were upset over what they viewed as the second-class status of Singaporeans as citizens of the soon-to-be-formed Malaysia. Among other things, Singapore had proportionately fewer Federal Assembly seats than it deserved by population. For the PAP, time was getting short; the merger was supposed to be established at the end of August 1963. And the Tunku, wary about the communist threat in the predominantly Chinese-populated Singapore, was still insistent that the threat be neutralised before the merger could proceed.

Operation Coldstore

GEB was privy to these fractious meetings with each side accusing the other of protecting their own interests and arguing over how responsibility for the pre-emptive arrests should be presented to the public. The Special Branch was pressed for more information and was put in charge of drawing up a list of suspects. During the meetings, GEB spoke only when asked for an opinion, but the questions would come fast and furious in the run-up to Operation Coldstore.

In one ISC meeting in September 1962, Toh Chin Chye, then Acting Prime Minister, asked him how he thought the Chinese electorate would react to arrests of Barisan Sosialis members. "His assessment of the feeling among the Chinese-speaking people in Singapore was that by and large they did not think of the Barisan Sosialis as directed by the Malayan Communist Party, and did not associate them with a communist conspiracy," the minutes recorded.

It was a careful reply, giving no hint of his own views. In any case, the Special Branch produced paper after paper for the ISC on the security situation in Singapore, which led ultimately to a softening of the British position. Informers and agents had given evidence of Barisan Sosialis meetings, which indicated that the communists were prepared to resort to unconstitutional means to unseat the current government. The Special Branch, it seemed, had plenty of intelligence about the Communist United Front activities but it was uncertain about the degree of involvement of individuals or whether they should be labelled "communists".

The tipping point was the Brunei revolt, which broke out on 8 December 1962. It was said to be at the instigation of insurgents from the North Borneo National Army, which did not want a merger with Singapore, Malaya, Sarawak and North Borneo (today's Sabah) to form Malaysia. Indonesia, under the Sukarno government which was also against the merger, was said to be giving support to the revolt.

The rebels were, however, unable to achieve their aims of capturing the Sultan of Brunei, seizing the Brunei oil fields or taking European hostages. In less than 48 hours, the British put down the insurrection.

On the day after the news of the revolt had broken, the Barisan Sosialis issued a statement of support hailing the "popular uprising against colonialism" and urged Singapore and the Federation to make similar statements. GEB also reported seeing Lim Chin Siong with rebel leader A. M. Azahari in a restaurant at Dhoby Ghaut in Singapore, ostensibly discussing the buying and selling of weapons two days before the revolt.

The Barisan Sosialis' public statement was a move that sealed its fate. Five days later, on 13 December, the ISC was convened at the request of the Tunku. The minutes showed that Selkirk was changing tack. He said that new intelligence reports were "showing more clearly the extent of MCP control over Barisan Sosialis and that they had been taking a more militant stance in their public statements". The party's open support for the armed revolt in Brunei had also shown that they approved the use of force and "that there was a real threat that they might use it here".

The Federal and Singapore Special Branches were tasked with drawing up a list of names of those to be arrested and the case against them, as well as the organisations and publications to be proscribed. Lee wanted to include nine Barisan Sosialis assemblymen on the list, but this was on condition that the Federal government also took action against their pro-communist MPs. It was agreed that about 180 persons would be arrested by the Singapore Special Branch.

Pending the consent of the Tunku to the arrests of his MPs, the operation was to take place two days later, on Sunday morning at 2 am, 16 December 1962.

The planning came to naught. The Tunku threw a spanner in the works by refusing to arrest his own MPs, citing lack of evidence against them.

As the British scrambled to get the Federation back to the ISC table, one important event took place: On 20 January 1963, Indonesia declared its policy of Konfrontasi, or Confrontation, against Malaya. It moved from low-level anti-Malaya propaganda to armed incursions, bomb attacks and other subversive acts to destabilise states that were to be included in the new Malaysia. The attacks would escalate after the merger became a reality.

In the meantime, in the ISC, Lee Kuan Yew wanted three members of Ong Eng Guan's United People's Party arrested to stop the maverick politician, who had been elected in the Hong Lim by-election of 1961, from being a magnet for communist elements who might escape the dragnet. A cable telegram from Selkirk to the colonial secretary showed that GEB had reservations. "Director of Special Branch admitted however that he had been directed specifically by the Prime Minister to select several members of the UPP for arrests and it would never have occurred to the Special Branch to propose these names."

GEB also told Dennis Bloodworth, who authored *The Tiger and the Trojan Horse*, that Singapore had to "twist it a bit" in the crime sheets submitted to the ISC to have a "security justification" to detain a few people, such as trade unionist James Puthucheary, a founding member of the PAP who joined Lim Chin Siong to form Barisan Sosialis.

When the ISC next met on 1 February, there was a shorter arrest list of 169 people. Among those who got off the list were six Barisan assemblymen, because the Tunku would still not agree to arrest his own MPs. About 2 am the next day, more than 500 policemen from both Singapore and Johor formed 65 parties to fan out and locate the 169. By the end of the month-long round-up, 116 were in detention.

GEB told Bloodworth that he and his team were at the police officers' mess on the eve of Operation Coldstore for a formal party. When the party ended, all of them proceeded to the Police Training School in Mount Pleasant Road in their tuxedos. In fact, the black tie they wore was a good cover and they were still in their dinner jackets the next morning, after spending the night executing Coldstore.

He said in an interview with *The Straits Times* after his retirement in 1981:

> I did not and do not have any qualms about the operation. I went into the Special Branch with my eyes open. If the Barisan Sosialis and their friends had won, we would all have gone down.
>
> I did not think the ones detained were innocent. Yes, they might be foolish but they were certainly not innocent.

While most observers believe that the operation had broken the back of the communists in Singapore, Lee Kuan Yew was less optimistic and wanted more action. He was concerned that the Barisan Sosialis remnants would use even more aggressive tactics to show that it was still a force to be reckoned with.

All these tensions came to the fore at the first ISC meeting after Operation Coldstore, held in Kuala Lumpur on Friday, 26 April 1963. The account that follows is drawn from the minutes found in the declassified British files numbered DO/187/16: ISC (63). Singapore's National Archives has not yet opened access to the Special Branch's own files, held in Singapore.

At that first meeting, Lee said the Special Branch had been "conservative in suggesting the names of those who should be arrested". Lee thought that Lee Siew Choh, the Barisan Sosialis chairman, should have been included. Lee Siew Choh seemed to have been influenced by his leftist comrades in the Barisan Sosialis, he said. Goh Keng Swee agreed with him. GEB's response was laconic. He agreed that Lee Siew Choh had been "brought more and more into the Barisan Sosialis counsels since the end of 1962 and that he was now a committed 'front man'." One possible reading of GEB's comments: Lee Siew Choh's transformation was too recent for his name to make that 2 February arrest list.

Lee Siew Choh continued to carry the Barisan Sosialis flame, visiting the detainees at the Outram Prison, condemning their living conditions and denouncing the PAP's use of the "communist bogey" to stem its own fall in popular opinion. Besides losing the Hong Lim by-election, the PAP had also lost the Anson by-election in 1961, with David Marshall beating four other candidates.

Noting that four days before the ISC meeting, rioters had stormed City Hall to demand the release of those detained under Operation Coldstore, Lee Kuan Yew asked if this was the start of renewed activity by the Barisan Sosialis, since eight of its members had been arrested.

GEB was asked for his opinion: Did he believe the disturbances were premeditated? He replied that the "disturbances were premeditated, but not the riots." This was probably not what Lee Kuan Yew wanted to hear. Lee remarked that the demonstration was carefully planned with "sticks and bottles provided". There was also another crowd gathered and "ready" nearby.

GEB also said that Barisan Sosialis would find it incumbent to take a more aggressive stance or sponsor militant action to appease its followers. Although the City Hall riots had taken place, it had backed down on holding other demonstrations, he said, adding "if they continued in this way, their support will ebb away".

The ISC was put in a prickly position. It would be hard to marshal enough evidence to prosecute the Barisan Sosialis assemblymen in court. Using the PPSO would also give rise to questions about why they weren't snagged during Operation Coldstore. In the end, the ISC decided that PPSO arrests should only be made if they attempted to mount further violent demonstrations on May Day or after.

Professional or PAP stooge?

While there is scant information on GEB's work during Operation Coldstore, some facets of his professionalism can be gleaned from the Internal Security Council minutes following the dragnet. Whatever the reporting hierarchy, he was Singapore's man tasked with carrying out the vision of the elected government attempting to ride through the political, social and economic tumult. His responses were clinical at times, even at a slight variance from the line taken by his political master, but there is no evidence of toadying.

In an interview with *The Straits Times* in 1981, GEB described politics as a "fairly unsavoury business". His working principle was that civil servants had to recognise the will of the people vested in an elected government, and that policies had to change according to social and political conditions of the day. In his words, civil servants had to be "politicised". He made a distinction between being politically aware and politically involved. "There is a clear difference here. It is a difference between the practice and science of it. I was interested only in the science of it."

It may be safely said that his position was aligned with the basic ideology of the PAP: that law and order must be established first, so that the economic and social needs of the people can be met. Civil servants had to come out with analyses of the situation and work out the details for the action political leaders wanted.

In the same 1981 newspaper interview, GEB admitted that there could be occasions when the line between political and security considerations became blurred. "It was very difficult for the Special Branch to become overtly political. There might be minor areas of doubt about whether we were providing the government with political rather than security intelligence."

The ISC members, including Lee Kuan Yew, valued GEB's insights. In April 1963, when the Special Branch was criticised for what the British saw as "negligible results of the interrogations to date", Lee replied that the interrogations had yielded a good deal of corroboration though not any startling new evidence.

At the same meeting, the British members also criticised the Special Branch for the solitary confinement of 75 detainees of Operation Coldstore. Selkirk was doubtful that more significant information could be yielded through their interrogation that would outweigh the mounting criticism by the Opposition in the British House of Commons. He wanted them all out of their cells into the general prison population by the end of May as "Her Majesty's Government would not be able to defend long-term solitary confinement."

In this, GEB had the support of the Federation representative Ismail Abdul Rahman, who said that it would be useless to interrogate detainees released from solitary confinement as they would be able to compare notes with each other and decide on what they should say. "The Singapore government had to be guided by their Director of Special Branch and could not, in effect, tell him not to do his job," Ismail said.

GEB added that a sudden large release of those in solitary confinement would only encourage the other detainees to believe that if they held out long enough, they too would be able to get out of their cells.

Lee Kuan Yew objected to Selkirk's deadline of end-May, arguing that this would "handicap" the Special Branch in getting intelligence through interrogations. The compromise was to release them in stages, with the first batch timed before the arrival of three British Opposition members of parliament from the Labour Party in Singapore on 17 May 1963.

Solitary confinement continued to be an issue for the British over the next two ISC meetings. They were impatient that "very little had come out of the interrogations of those detained". GEB's response was that he lacked the manpower to process the material produced from interrogations. Besides resignations from officers who did not want to be associated with the arrests of communists, there were also those who were deemed sympathetic to the communist cause. Two years earlier, four senior Special Branch officials had to leave the service because they had contact with pro-communists such as Lim Chin Siong and Tan Lark Sye.

Post-Operation Coldstore

With Operation Coldstore in the bag and mop-up operations being planned, the stage was set for Singapore's merger with Malaya to form Malaysia. Although the merger became a reality on 16 September 1963, the Barisan Sosialis still acted as if the PAP and not the Federal government was in charge of the country. Strikes and demonstrations continued in Singapore, with protestors taking up political causes, such as the de-registration of Nanyang University founder Tan Lark Sye as a citizen.

The Singapore Special Branch, acting on Federal orders, moved swiftly to clamp down on Nanyang University demonstrators and trade unionists. Unlike previous operations, there was no need for any pussy-footing this time round. While the PAP government might have qualms taking actions that would rile the majority-Chinese electorate, the Malay-dominated Federal government in Kuala Lumpur had no problem flexing its muscles. This raid came to be known as Operation Pechah. It took place eight months after Operation Coldstore and three weeks after the September general elections. Included in the even longer list of more than 170 names were two Barisan Sosialis assemblymen, three failed Barisan Sosialis candidates and leading trade union activists.

Merger meant, however, that the Singapore Special Branch was a subset of the Malaysian office. Unlike the Singapore version, the Malaysian Special Branch was conceptualised more like a police outfit than an intelligence unit. Lee Kuan Yew was consistently urged by Claude Fenner, the Malaysian Inspector-General of Police, to go through the proper channels—that is, Singapore Police Commissioner Le Cain—if he wanted to obtain information. Lee, on the other hand, wanted to be able, "from time to time to speak directly to Bogaars although of course he would inform Le Cain what had taken place". It appeared that he did so frequently, calling GEB for information and insights to understand how the security situation affected politics. For Lee, security and politics were inextricably linked. This was something GEB understood well.

By all accounts, the Special Branches on both sides of the Causeway got on well. GEB had a friendly disposition, travelled often to Malaysia and had made friends with his counterparts and the politicians there. Of the civil servants of the era, he probably had the most interaction with the Malaysian leadership circles, travelling as part of the Singapore delegation for meetings in Cameron Highlands, Kuala Lumpur and Johor.

While the communist threat was somewhat contained in the merger years, the Special Branch would find it more difficult to deal with another threat: communal forces bent on taking political power.

VI

Dousing Communal Fires

The year 1964 was the bloodiest year in Singapore since the war. Because Federal elections were to be held that year, politicians were unabashedly playing one community against the other in fiery speeches to gain electoral support. The largest and deadliest riot occurred on 21 July 1964, after some fierce rhetoric by Malaysian United Malays National Organisation (UMNO) politicians alleging that the situation of the Malays in Singapore was even worse now, with the PAP in charge, than it was during the Japanese Occupation.

The Jawi-script Malay newspaper *Utusan Melayu* published a slew of articles condemning Lee Kuan Yew and lamenting the position of the Malays. Simmering tensions came to a boil on 20 July. The next day, racial riots broke out during the celebratory procession of Prophet Mohammad's birthday attended by 20,000 Muslims near Kallang Gasworks, a Chinese-dominated area.

Worried about trouble breaking out during the celebrations, Lee Kuan Yew had earlier sounded out Commissioner of Police John Le Cain and GEB for their views on this possibility. According to Albert Lau, writing in *A Moment of Anguish,* the police replied in the negative while the Special Branch had "received unconfirmed reports that the Malays in the southern and city areas were expecting trouble on Prophet Mohammed's birthday and that they had been told to wait for instructions."

The intelligence gathered by the Special Branch was proven correct. The flare was lit when a Chinese threw a bottle into the crowd of Muslims. A Chinese policeman who tried to intervene in the resultant melee was himself assaulted. All hell broke loose after. The day ended with four deaths and 178 injured.

GEB and Le Cain briefed Lee Kuan Yew at the police headquarters in Pearl's Hill that evening and permission was sought from the Federal side to impose a curfew. But riots still continued in various parts of the island. By the end of July, 23 persons had died and 454 others were injured. Out of the 3,568 persons arrested during the riots, 715 were charged in court and 945 were placed under preventive detention.

Despite the crackdown, riots broke out again in September after the death of a Malay trishaw rider in Geylang, resulting in 13 fatalities and 106 persons injured. Out of the 1,439 persons arrested, 154 were charged in court and another 268 were placed under preventive detention.

The PAP and the UMNO-dominated Alliance laid charges at each other's doors. A Committee of Inquiry was set up to examine the cause of the riot. The conclusions, however, have never been published. Instead, both Singapore and Malaysia officially blamed Indonesian provocateurs for causing the September riots. They said they believed the riots were part of Indonesia's Konfrontasi policy aimed at weakening Malaysia.

Diplomatic cables, however, showed that GEB found little evidence pointing clearly to Indonesian involvement. "Although he agreed that the riots owed something to Indonesian influence, Bogaars discounted the theory of direct Indonesian instigation of which he said there was no evidence at all," said W. A. Luscombe of the Australian High Commission in Kuala Lumpur.

Still, there was a plausible inference of an Indonesian hand, given the intensification of Konfrontasi. On 27 July, Sukarno had announced a "Ganyang Malaysia", or "Crush Malaysia", campaign because he saw a unified Malaysia as the start of a new imperialism spearheaded by the British. Others, however, believed that Konfrontasi was launched to take the Indonesian people's attention away from the country's own domestic travails.

Two days after the Federation of Malaysia was formed on 16 September, rioters burned the British Embassy in Jakarta and ransacked the homes of Singapore representatives and the Singapore trade office. Cross-border incursions into Sarawak and Sabah, which ceased to be British territories, escalated. Attention was shifted to Peninsular Malaysia and Singapore. Paratroopers were dropped on the peninsula and infiltrators started bombing places. Indonesia's navy tried to land along the shores and shoot-outs at sea with the British took place.

Singapore's first bomb attack occurred just eight days after it joined Malaysia. The wave of bombings killed seven people and injured 50 others. The most serious incident was the MacDonald House bombing, on 10 March 1965, in which three were killed and 33 others injured. Two Indonesian marines were hanged for their part in the bombing.

Terrorism had come to Singapore.

Besides dealing with internal extremists, the Special Branch now had to position itself to deal with outside elements, from another sovereign country. For civil servants conditioned to think largely in terms of Singapore's internal problems, this was a new arena. They had to consider geopolitical forces, diplomatic arrangements and the vagaries of Cold War politics. GEB said in *Towards Tomorrow* that

Indonesian Konfrontasi had helped to weaken the "insular attitude" bred in the colonial years.

One consolation was that the British still provided the security shield and took the brunt of Konfrontasi. In 1963, the Malayan armed forces were limited in strength, consisting of eight infantry battalions with support groups, a navy designed largely for coastal patrol and an air force capable of performing only transport functions.

The British forces had five British and Gurkha battalions in Borneo in May 1963, two carriers with airborne marines on intermittent service, and a commando ship based at Hong Kong; commando groups at Singapore and Kuching; various Royal Navy vessels, including a cruiser; and Royal Air Force units including Canberras, Javelins, Hunters, various transport units and helicopters.

Konfrontasi eased over the months because of internal divisions within the Jakarta government. In what was later known as the 30th September Movement, several top army generals were kidnapped and murdered on 1 October 1965 in an attempted coup purportedly executed by the Indonesian Communist Party.

The coup was crushed on the same day by General Suharto and his army. President Sukarno, discredited for his alleged association with the party, relinquished power to Suharto in March 1966. This heralded the New Order. It was a more amenable regime. After talks began in May 1966, both Malaysia and Indonesia eventually signed a peace treaty and agreed to end the confrontation.

Even before this was achieved, however, Malaysian premier Tunku Abdul Rahman started changing his mind about having Singapore within the Federation. He had reluctantly agreed to its inclusion because he saw it necessary to have control over the Chinese-dominated country, which seemed in danger of falling into communist hands.

The danger turned out to be more primeval than ideological. The consequence of the merger was a change in demographics. With the inclusion of Singapore, the Chinese now formed 44.1 per cent of Malaysia, up from 37.2 per cent in 1957. The proportion of Malays fell from 49.8 per cent to 43.2 per cent. The Tunku had governed as head of an alliance of race-based parties and made no bones about the United Malays National Organisation being the dominant player.

The Alliance Party and PAP politicians were at loggerheads with each other from the start, not least because of the PAP's pursuit of a Malaysian Malaysia rather than a Malay-dominated one. Both sides made political forays into each other's territory, despite promises that they would stick to their own corner. Malay "ultras" such as UMNO's Khir Johari and Syed Jaafar Albar called on Malays in Singapore to unite, believing that the PAP would relegate the status of the Malay community to the fringes. The PAP, on the other hand, was pushing itself forward as a replacement for the Malayan Chinese Association, the Chinese partner of the Alliance.

In June 1965, GEB, who had access to the Malaysian Special Branch in Kuala Lumpur, informed Lee Kuan Yew that the Malaysian "ultras" were trying to make a case for his arrest. Even though this was denied by the Malaysians and could be a ploy to rumble Singapore, it demonstrated the degree of estrangement between two sides of the Causeway.

The Tunku decided to cut the cord and the PAP side was left scrambling to secure favourable terms for Separation, at least one that could allow Singapore to develop economically, trade freely and with security assurances in place.

Internal security was still an issue, given that communal tensions do not respect borders.

On 13 May 1969, parts of Malaysia imploded when the opposition Chinese-based parties made inroads into the Malaysian Parliament in the general election. Malays, who already feared the predominance of the Chinese in the economy, wondered if the Chinese were now also eyeing political hegemony. By the time the riots were over, official figures said 196 people had been killed, 6,000 made homeless and more than 700 buildings destroyed or damaged. The Malaysian government declared a state of emergency and suspended Parliament until 1971.

Many theories have surfaced about how the riots started. Was it a spontaneous combustion among the Malays who were taunted by the Chinese supporters of the opposition Democratic Action Party and Gerakan parties? In his book, *13 May: Before and After*, the Tunku blamed the opposition parties for the violence, as well as the influence of the communists, and thought that the incidents were sparked off by Chinese communist youths. Yet another theory was that it was an UMNO plot to oust the Tunku, who was viewed as too soft on non-Malays.

The communal troubles spilled into Singapore as the different communities started viewing each other with suspicion. Fuelled by rumours, Malay mobs and Chinese triads in Singapore began attacking one another.

The riots started when Chinese plotters from a Malaysian triad society collaborated with members of the Ang Soon Tong Triad Society and Ji It Triad Society to attack Malay residents of Kampong Kedah, which was near Seletar Air Base. On 31 May, gangsters from the Ji It Triad Society killed a Malay woman who was walking along Jalan Ubi with her daughter. The Malays retaliated on 1 June, when thugs from the Black Hawk Malay secret society set fire to a Chinese-owned sundry shop in Geylang. The seven-day clashes left four people dead and some 80 injuries. The Special Branch, now known as the Internal Security Department, rounded up more than 700 people for questioning in the aftermath of these clashes.

By now, GEB was the Permanent Secretary of the Interior and Defence Ministry, with an overview of the Internal Security Department. How he handled the crisis raised doubts about his ability to control the security forces. Had GEB's political antenna let him down?

VII

Building an Army
from Scratch

The ninth of August 1965 began peculiarly for GEB and a few senior civil servants. They were summoned to the prime minister's official residence, Sri Temasek, at the Istana. Lee Kuan Yew told them about the news that would break at noon—Singapore's separation from Malaysia. The civil servants, including Sim Kee Boon, Stanley Stewart, Hon Sui Sen, and Attorney-General Ahmad Ibrahim, hung around to hear the broadcast on radio before going back to their respective offices.

GEB thought he would continue to work in the Special Branch in an independent Singapore, especially since the prime minister himself had asked him about its ability to quell disturbances arising from a split. GEB himself had some initial worries about Malay extremism being practised by the Malaysian politicians to placate Malays in Singapore who might feel "abandoned" by them. But he had hardly warmed his seat that day when he was summoned to see his old boss, Goh Keng Swee. He was asked to head a new ministry in charge of internal and external security under Goh. He said yes.

According to author Tan Siok Sun of *Goh Keng Swee: A Portrait*, GEB was stunned by the offer but was unhesitating about taking it up.

> The newly appointed perm sec's input was almost immediate. During a brainstorming session at the Fullerton Building office, it was Bogaars who suggested naming the new Ministry the "Ministry of the Interior and Defence (MID)" rather than just merely "Ministry of the Interior" or "Ministry of Defence". He further explained himself by suggesting that the words "interior" and "defence", when placed together possessed a rather mysterious and even sinister connotation, with which GKS laughingly concurred.

Dr Goh's decision to marry police and military work made sense, given the geographical size of Singapore and its fledgling military. Policemen could also serve as senior officers to supplement the military ranks. Also, the emphasis in those days was on quelling internal unrest, rather than dealing with external threats.

"When we came out of Malaysia, we had just these two battalions, the two SIRs. One was still doing some service in East Malaysia, the other was in Singapore. And that was all we had, really, to build our defence forces on," GEB recalled in a 1984 television documentary, *25 Years in Retrospect*.

The two regular battalions were the First Singapore Infantry Regiment (1SIR), set up in 1957, and the Second Singapore Infantry Regiment (2SIR), formed in 1962. There were also the Vigilante Corps and the Singapore Volunteer Corps. To boost the numbers, recruitment drives were held to beef up a new People's Defence Force. But the Singapore government was soon to realise that a small corps of elite soldiers complemented by volunteers would not suffice. At what was said to be at the prompting of its Israeli military advisors, conscription for a citizen army was deemed necessary.

On Separation, Singapore was hardly defenceless. The British still had a significant presence on the island, with 28,800 uniformed personnel, 2,000 civilians and 3,300 Gurkhas, as of April 1967. They also occupied the military bases such as Sembawang Naval Base, Changi Air Base, Seletar Air Base, Sembawang Air Base and Tengah Air Base. Together, the bases accounted for 12 per cent of the island's total land area. Such an extensive British presence, however, was soon to prove more of a headache than a comfort.

Malaysian intransigence

The Ministry of Interior and Defence, which was later split into the Home Affairs and Defence ministries, was first set up in rooms at the Ministry of Social Affairs in Empress Place. It moved to Pearl's Hill in November 1965.

Now that GEB was the civil servant in charge of both internal and external security, his Special Branch portfolio had to go to someone else. GEB recommended Tay Seow Huah, a family friend who was then with the PSA, to his boss Dr Goh. In Tay's time, the Special Branch would morph to become the Internal Security Department, dealing only with domestic troubles while the Defence Ministry took care of outside threats.

While much has been said about the building of the Singapore Armed Forces to its powerful state today, less is known about the tensions simmering after Separation between the two countries over who was really in charge of defence. Malaysia had the military wherewithal compared to Singapore and was keen to keep overall watch over defence arrangements. In fact, it insisted on calling the shots.

An early sign was its insistence on keeping Malaysian troops on Singapore soil. When the Singapore soldiers from 2SIR returned from their East Malaysia sojourn, the Malaysian government refused to vacate the Holland Road Camp, where its own infantry was housed, for the returnees. They argued that Malaysia was responsible for the defence of Singapore and that the defence of the two territories was inseparable.

They pointed to Article Five of the Separation agreement, which covered defence issues. This said that Singapore and Malaysia agreed to "enter into a treaty on external defence and mutual assistance" providing that several conditions were met:

- the establishment of a Joint Defence Council.
- Malaysia would assist Singapore with external defence and Singapore would provide military units for this purpose.
- Singapore would give the Malaysian government the right to continue to maintain the bases and other facilities used by its military forces in Singapore and would allow Malaysia to use these bases and facilities as the Malaysian government may consider necessary.
- Both sides would undertake not to enter into treaties with third parties which might be "detrimental to the independence and defence of the territory of the other party".

Among other things, Malaysia interpreted the third condition to mean that Singapore was obliged to house its troops or provide suitable premises, and that this right remained with the Malaysian government. The stalemate was only broken when the British vacated Khatib Camp in March 1966 for the Malaysians. It would take another 18 months for the Malaysian infantry to leave for home. In the meantime, GEB had to borrow tents from the British to house Singapore's own soldiers at Farrer Park.

Security expert Tim Huxley said in his book, *Defending the Lion City*, that while the provisions seemed to lay the foundations for continuing extremely close bilateral defence links, "in practice, such ties did not endure for long after Separation".

The Joint Defence Council comprising Singapore and Malaysian officials was a non-starter, especially since Singapore's sole representative was overwhelmed by the number of Malaysians. Meetings were sporadic and it was also clear the Malaysians were making decisions unilaterally for Singapore and setting not just the defence agenda, but also the economic agenda. Singapore withdrew from the council in March 1966.

When Indonesia announced in April 1966 that it would recognise Singapore as an independent state, Malaysia objected to Singapore making any response, arguing that Konfrontasi had not been formally concluded. Singapore leaders sought to assure Malaysia that the island would not allow herself to be used in the Indonesian confrontation of Malaysia. Nor would she allow herself to be a wedge between the two countries. Singapore was only interested in trading with Indonesia.

But that mercantilist objective was shot down by Malaysia too.

The Singapore–Indonesia barter trade had been an issue since merger days. Malaysia had argued that such trade was a cover for Indonesians to infiltrate the Federation to do damage. Its position was vindicated in some way, as the two Indonesians who bombed MacDonald House had entered the country as traders. New proposals by Singapore to limit barter trade with Indonesia through Pulau Senang were also met with disapproval. At one point, Malaysia threatened to use the Royal Malaysian Navy to blockade the offshore island. Dr Goh, as Minister for Interior and Defence, reached the stage when he was wondering if he should make public the Malaysian-Indonesian clandestine trading taking place in huge volumes at its ports to demonstrate its hypocrisy. He was advised against it.

GEB was privy to the bilateral wrangles taking place at the ministerial level. In his correspondence with the British, who took a determined interest in defence matters, it was clear that the Malaysians were asking for deference in all matters, even having a say in agreements that Singapore signed with third parties that had nothing to do with defence.

Both countries had objectives which were diametrically opposite. Malaysia was most keen to conclude a defence treaty with Singapore incorporating the terms of Article Five, which would give it command and control of the military. Singapore, on the other hand, wanted movement on Article Six, which sought economic co-operation. Its ultimate objective of having a Common Market with Malaysia, even during the merger days, hardly made any headway. Singapore had difficulty securing pioneer status from Kuala Lumpur for Singaporean companies. Then there were other new sovereignty issues, such as immigration and the presence of huge numbers of Malaysians working in Singapore and vice versa.

Minutes of a particularly tense meeting in Singapore on 19 May 1966 between the two sides showed the wide breach over the issues. Led by Hon Sui Sen, chairman of the Economic Development Board (EDB), and attended by GEB and Sim Kee Boon, the Singapore side faced off the Malaysian side led by Permanent Secretary for Foreign Affairs Ghazali Shafie, who was in high dudgeon at Singapore's proposal to allow an Indonesian trade mission on its shores.

Even as Ghazali acknowledged Singapore's sovereignty, the "special relationship" obliged Singapore to seek consultations before signing agreements with any country, he said. Ghazali also tried to expedite the signing of a defence treaty, by noting that there was already a de facto arrangement with Malaysian troops in Singapore. GEB replied that the troops were there with the consent of the Singapore government, which would rather have them out.

Singapore, however, was not pressing the issue lest it strained relations further, he added.

Neither side would give an inch as each sought to get the other to agree to settle their own priorities first. Ultimately, the idea of a defence treaty petered out and both sides pursued their own economic development and defence strategies.

All these activities were taking place against the backdrop of the proxy war that was happening in Southeast Asia. Claiming that North Vietnam attacked its naval vessels in the Gulf of Tonkin in August 1964, the United States threw its support behind South Vietnam against the communist North Vietnamese regime that was backed by the Soviet Union and China. The domino theory was in vogue then. If South Vietnam fell to the North Vietnamese, how long would it be before continental Southeast Asia came under communist domination?

The flip side, however, was that the increasing American presence in the region spurred economic growth in Singapore. After the war started in November 1955, the Americans used Singapore as a petroleum-refining centre for the war and also set up the Lockheed Corporation here to repair and maintain military aircraft deployed to Vietnam. In 1967, 15 per cent of Singapore's national income came from military procurements by the United States for Vietnam. Gross domestic product growth reached a peak of 13.9 per cent in 1970.

Recruiting the reluctant

Beginning in early 1966, the MID mounted Operations Boxer and Boxer II, involving stepped-up recruitment and training to rapidly boost regular personnel strength. By the end of the year, more than 1,100 new regular soldiers recruited in Singapore had been trained, restoring the infantry regiments and artillery battalions almost to full strength. Malaysia's belligerence had only reinforced the

Singapore government's belief that a strong defence force had to be built quickly. According to Huxley, a confidential defence plan was finalised by September 1966, almost certainly with Israeli advice, and envisaged the army's expansion to 12 battalions within a decade, an objective which could only be achieved through conscription.

The Singapore government was mindful that locals did not take to the idea of having their sons turn to soldiering. It was not a glamorous calling among the Chinese-educated, and even less among the English-educated. Said GEB in the 1984 TV documentary:

> Looking back, I think the biggest problem was to convince those of our young men who had educated themselves quite well in the institutes and tertiary educational institutions that they had a special role to play in building up the defence force. That they had to withhold somewhat their expectations of a large income because, at that time, the economy was just beginning to move off. And that they had to defer their expectations for a few years and help build up a strong and viable defence force.
>
> That was I think for us in the beginning in the early days of the Ministry of Defence, the biggest problem.

There were also the memories of the Anti-National Service Riots of 1954, stirred by the communists, after Governor William Goode announced that males between 18 and 20 years of age would be drafted. Students from the Chinese schools had refused to register and took to the streets despite concessions made to exempt certain categories of residents.

The first inkling of conscription came in November 1966, when Dr Goh announced that from 1 January 1967, all newly appointed public servants, subject to medical fitness, would have to do a stint of full-time military service. In February 1967, Dr Goh tabled legislation in Parliament to amend the National Service Ordinance (which had originally been passed by the British in 1953). The next month, Parliament approved the National Service (Amendment) Bill. Some 9,000 male youths born between the six-month period of 1 January 1949 and 30 June 1949 would be called up for National Service.

Reactions to the call-up were mixed. Street demonstrations were staged by up to 300 people who opposed the call-up. There were also protests by Chinese middle school students on 27 March 1967. But the disturbances were nowhere near the scale of those launched more than a decade previous.

There was another factor: The call-up had the support of the University of Singapore Student Union as well as the Singapore Chinese Chamber of Commerce, which led the effort to convince the Chinese-speaking community to let their sons register. By mid-April 1967, more than 90 per cent of the 9,000 young men eligible for National Service had registered. About 900 served as full-time National Servicemen.

Herman Hochstadt, director of manpower at the MID at that time, recalled how GEB organised successful open houses at army camps and send-off parties at community centres. A whole public relations campaign had been launched with flyers and brochures invoking pride and patriotism as well as glamour: one brochure featured a soldier in a red sports car.

Even as the National Service drive started taking off, there came another reason for urgency: In July 1967, the British announced that it would withdraw its troops from its ex-colonies by the mid-1970s. Singapore already had some idea that the British would leave, especially after the Labour Party took power in Britain. Denis Healey, the Defence Secretary, had hinted as much to Lee Kuan Yew when he was in Singapore in July 1966.

The formal announcement threw the newly independent ex-colonies into a panic. For Singapore, the British troop withdrawal would leave the fledgling Republic bereft of air and naval protection. On the economic front, the British military bases, which directly employed 40,000 workers, were contributing over 20 per cent of Singapore's gross national product. To add to the consternation, just four months later, the mid-1970s deadline was moved up to March 1971. The British cited squeezed finances which had led to the devaluation of the pound, and the massive expense of maintaining its military bases as reasons for the earlier pull-out.

The British knew full well the impact of troop withdrawal on newly independent countries. "Singapore, in particular, would find it impossible to cope with such a timetable, which would bring economic disaster and her future alignment would almost inevitably be affected," said a July 1967 cable from the Secretary of State for Commonwealth Affairs Herbert Bowden. Lee Kuan Yew and Tunku Abdul Rahman tried to delay the move, using all sorts of threats, including putting out suggestions to let the Japanese use the British bases. But their overtures and pleas only led to a postponement of the withdrawal from March to November 1971.

At the same time, the Americans were being worn down by domestic sentiment against the Vietnam War and seemed intent on withdrawing from the Indochinese theatre sooner rather than later. Declassified cables from the US embassy in Singapore shed light on the concerns that GEB had should this take place. He had asked embassy officials about Washington's position if "the fingers were on our throats". Would the US provide military hardware or believe that Singapore was already "arming to the teeth"?

After Konfrontasi with Indonesia had ended and the Sukarno regime had been replaced, GEB was concerned that the fledgling Suharto regime might feel compelled to stage another foreign adventure in the style of his predecessor to draw attention away from domestic troubles. Even the possibility of this would deter businessmen and investors, especially as the British pull-out meant that there would be no naval or air cover.

He was also concerned about communist activity in the north of Malaysia along the Thai border, which could spill into the rest of Malaysia. He did not think the communists were interested in taking over Singapore as they seemed to be adhering to China's line to take over the rural areas first before hitting the towns. This would still lead to concerns about refugees flooding into Singapore and the Chinese community insisting that Singapore hew to a certain position.

Staffing up the force

Writing in *One of a Kind: Remembering SAFTI's First Batch*, retired colonel Ramchandran Menon said that the creative process for the SAF was "deceptively simple", like the flowcharts of a later generation. Creating the SAF

> would mean a massive injection of officers and NCOs [non-commissioned officers] into the current establishment ... so start recruiting and training; that would in turn require a super-efficient training institution; so clear out the people in about one tenth of the total land area of the country and build one; many trainers would be required, so strip the existing military establishments of their best and brightest, mobilise and second others and train them to be trainers.
>
> These decisions were not recorded elsewhere as historically significant, but they were: the pieces fell into place with remarkable cohesion—might one say, with military precision?

As Permanent Secretary, GEB would have had to see through this process. Over two years, the MID was organised into four divisions. Besides a General Staff division, there were Manpower, Logistics and Finance, and Home Affairs divisions. In addition to the ground forces, he would have had to look at the other arenas of defence. The Singapore Naval Volunteer Force was established in January 1966 and the Singapore Air Defence Command two years later. In 1975, they morphed into the Republic of Singapore Navy and the Republic of Singapore Air Force respectively.

According to Menon, the MID was given carte blanche to raid the establishment for manpower to staff the positions rapidly opening up in the ministry. Bosses stood aside. "Not many would have wanted to test Dr Goh's patience. In most cases, however, the name of George Bogaars, the Permanent Secretary of MID, handpicked by Dr Goh and a legend in his own time, would have sufficed."

It was a far cry from the early days when GEB would be personally asking for the loan of rifles from the British or making accommodation arrangements for the Israeli advisors who had answered Singapore's appeal for help.

There was plenty of weapons-buying too: A squadron of British-made Hawker Hunter fighters (with local pilots sent to train in Britain), British-made Bloodhound surface-to-air missiles for a minimal ground-based anti-aircraft defence and new naval patrol vessels to guard the Singapore Strait and port limits.

To train officers and NCOs, the Singapore Armed Forces Training Institute (SAFTI) was established, initially in a vacant primary school in Jurong in February 1966. It took in its first batch the same month for the first Instructors' Preparatory Course, developed by the Israeli advisors. The first course was almost derailed after a fortnight because of antagonism between the locals and Israelis. The locals were displeased at having to drill repeatedly with self-loading rifles and other field work that they were already familiar with. GEB met with the class and gave them a talking-to. Training continued after a two-week suspension to review the syllabus.

In the meantime, 331 acres of land at Pasir Laba were cleared of farms and became a single-storey, functional building with facilities such as a medical centre, an Olympic-sized swimming pool, auditoriums and an ammunition store. The institute was opened by Dr Goh on 18 June 1966.

Menon remarked in his book that the answer as to how Singapore had the money for its defence could only come from Dr Goh. It couldn't have been easy. In fact, it prompted a Cabinet reshuffle with Goh Keng Swee and Finance Minister Lim Kim San exchanging portfolios in 1967. The Cabinet reshuffle statement said:

> The Prime Minister considers it advantageous that the role of the two Ministers be reversed. The Minister for Finance, in his new capacity as Minister of Defence, will be able to assess at Defence Ministry level the priorities of the claims being made on the Ministry of Finance. Mr Lim Kim San had not supported a number of such claims in his capacity as Finance Minister. Dr Goh, as Minister for Finance, will be able to weigh the total claims of the Ministry of Defence on the budget as against the claims by other Ministries and in the context of the development of the whole economy.

It is doubtful whether this switch led to any reassessment on the defence budget or not; in fact there had been an exponential hike. The budget for defence amounted to $16.25 million in 1965/66. For 1970/71, this was $51.4 million, moving up to $100 million in the following financial year, although it must be noted that by 1971, the budget for defence was calculated differently from the previous year when it was still under the MID. Defence took up 15.72 per cent of the budget by then.

According to Philip Yeo, the Defence Ministry no longer had to itemise what it needed to buy when he was its Permanent Secretary between September 1979 and December 1985. He told the author, "I had a block budget." While itemised budgets are a thing of the past, he referred to one piece of history that has withstood the test of time—the MID vehicle licence plate despite the ministry's name change. "Because how do you say MOD? Not very nice, so we refused it."

Another innovation that GEB introduced, which incidentally casts a different light on him: He included and enhanced the role of women in defence matters. Mrs Jaya Mohideen, a career diplomat and Singapore's ambassador to Finland, was the only woman of the 15 recruited into the Administrative Service in May 1967 and was assigned to the Manpower Division in the MID. When she was 22, she was appointed as the MID's chief of public affairs. "Not only was I very young and inexperienced, but I was a woman in a daunting male environment. George Bogaars had the patience to be my teacher and guiding light. Never once did I feel that being a woman was a disadvantage," she told the author. She also recalled that Louis Kraar, Asia correspondent for *Time* and *Fortune* at that time, told her that she was the only woman Head of Public Affairs in any Ministry of Defence he had ever met.

Operationally ready

By 1969, Singapore's National Day Parade was able to feature a procession of tanks and armoured vehicles for the first time. This show of military strength marked the beginnings of a credible defence force.

Bereft of British protection, new defence arrangements had to be drawn up, especially with the on-going war in Indochina. Britain and its four ex-colonies, now part of the Commonwealth, decided to make a pact to defend against perceived aggression from Indonesia and the rise of communism in Vietnam. In 1970, under the auspices of the Five Power Defence Arrangements comprising Singapore, Malaysia, Australia, New Zealand and Britain, the Singapore Armed Forces participated in its first large-scale military exercise, named Bersatu Padu, in the state of Terengganu.

Writing in his memoirs, *The Accidental Diplomat*, Maurice Baker, then High Commissioner to Malaysia, recalled that Lim Kim San and GEB were there to witness the exercise but the British helicopter pilot dropped them off in the wrong part of the jungle. They stayed put, wondering if they would be captured by "enemy" or "friendly forces" involved in the exercise. They were found by a search party after the organisers realised that they had not turned up for the exercise. This anecdote aside, the SAF's 900 men did themselves proud, fighting against more experienced foreign military forces, said Baker.

On the defence front, GEB was most associated with the setting up of today's SAFTI. Mickey Chiang, author of *SAF and 30 Years of National Service*, recalled being brought on a tour of SAFTI in 1969:

> Mr Bogaars spoke cordially with the officers: "You have many shortages, but we are doing the best that we can," he said. "Do you know how very difficult it is to obtain your AR15 rifles? They are sending us one case at a time! When we receive one case of rifles there is celebration in MID HQ."
>
> As he looked around the ring of sunburnt faces, he made an observation that rang true. "Outside, we have got Chinese, Malays, Indians and Eurasians of different colours. Here in the SAF there is only one colour—dark brown. We are Singaporeans, never forget that."

Procurement of those AR15 rifles, produced by Colt Industries, would cease to be a problem as Chartered Industries, set up in 1967, would be manufacturing them.

GEB himself said in an interview with the *Management Development* newsletter in 1981 that SAFTI was a source of pride for him.

> There are a few things that I think make me feel a little bit more satisfied. One of them was SAFTI. I felt I really did something there. There was nothing and you built up an Institute, and that began producing officers who then manned the whole of the Armed Forces and provided the officers cadre for the Armed Forces.
>
> I think SAFTI has stood the test of time. I don't think SAFTI has changed much today from what it was when it was first established. There are a few things more here and there, but basically it is much the same. That's the kind of thing one looks back on and says, okay, when the last nail is knocked into

your coffin, those are the things you are satisfied with. The other things are a little bit more intangible.

While he looked back on his defence stint with pride, not everybody thought he did a good job.

VIII

The Civil Servant as Public Manager

A newspaper editorial published on 12 August 1970 in *The Straits Times* said GEB's MID stint had "not been a complete success", an appellation that he said in a post-retirement interview "really hurt.... How could that be said when I had helped build up a defence force which had not existed before?" The editorial said the Cabinet was strengthened after a reshuffle due to changes and promotions in the Civil Service, and notably GEB's movement out of the MID. "I left because of circumstances I can't even now discuss," said GEB in a 1981 interview. "In fact, Finance Minister Hon Sui Sen, to whose ministry I went, asked me if I would like him to reply to that editorial on my behalf though he knew I wouldn't want to."

GEB moved out of the MID in 1970. At the same time, the MID was split into the Defence (which was returned to Dr Goh's care while out-going Defence Minister Lim Kim San went to the Education Ministry) and Home Affairs ministries, testimony to the increased size of the portfolio. The Special Branch had already been re-named the Internal Security Department and it reported to the

Home Affairs Minister, who was Ong Pang Boon as a result of the Cabinet reshuffle.

There could have been another reason for the move. GEB was in charge of the racial mix of the armed forces. Senior officers had been told to thin out the number of Malays in its recruitment drive because they were already over-represented in the uniformed services. Perhaps Bogaars had been remiss in checking the list of Malay inductees.

In *From Third World to First: The Singapore Story*, then Prime Minister Lee Kuan Yew had questioned the racial mix of military recruits in the aftermath of the 1969 race riots. He thought there were too many Malays.

> I wanted to be sure that the police and army were not weakened by communal pulls.... I also wanted an explanation why so many Malay soldiers were deployed in Geylang Serai where a Chinese minority would have been more reassured by a mixed-race force.
>
> George Bogaars, then permanent secretary of the defence ministry and one of our most trusted officers, had been director of the Special Branch where he learnt to distrust the Chinese-educated. He preferred Malays when recruiting non-commissioned officers and warrant officers for the SAF to train our national servicemen, believing the Chinese-educated were prone to Chinese chauvinism and communism.

Political scientist Alon Peled from The Hebrew University of Jerusalem gave the racial mix as a reason for GEB's departure. In his 1998 book, *A Question of Loyalty: Military Manpower Policy in Multi-ethnic States*, Peled cited interviews with Lim Kim San and Colonel James Aeria which suggested GEB had to leave because of his "loss of control".

Ask Seah Kia Ger however, who was then in the MID, and he would declare himself puzzled by the description of GEB as "anti-Chinese educated". Himself a graduate of Nanyang University, Seah recalled how GEB had intervened to save a Chinese-educated clerk's career because his superiors complained that his English was not up to scratch. "Mr Bogaars said that they were expecting him to use the language at the same level as someone who was English-educated. They should have sent him for some English language courses instead of expecting him to perform better in English."

The perks of public service

GEB's effort and devotion in the early days of Singapore and the Federation received their due.

He received the Meritorious Service Medal as well as the Malaysia medal in 1962. The citation which went with his first award described him as "an able and efficient administrator setting exemplary standards of work and devotion to duty" and whose "stout-hearted" qualities inspired his colleagues. That for the Malaysia medal read: "His intelligent approach to and assessment of security problems contributed a great deal to the peace and security of the State and helped to create the right atmosphere and make it easier for the orderly progress and entry of the State into Malaysia."

Five years later, the Singapore government awarded him the Distinguished Service Medal. He was described as "the archetype civil servant needed in the Republic of Singapore—politically perceptive, professionally versatile and morally courageous." It added that he had "administrative skills, untiring energy and devotion to duty that enabled the Ministry to develop, in a short time, into an effective instrument of control and supervision over the rapidly expanding defence forces of the Republic."

In 1968, GEB was appointed Head of Civil Service, a position he held till 1975. It was a stupendous rise, although it didn't come with an immediate salary raise as the 1959 austerity drive in the Civil Service was in place and would remain till 1972. Instead, the government compensated its top civil servants in 1969 by giving them a car.

GEB was just one of two senior civil servants who got a Mercedes Benz 280. At Superscale A, GEB and Howe Yoon Chong, then a Permanent Secretary at the Ministry of National Development and also chairman of the HDB, were making $3,000 a month in all. This compared terribly with the $10,000-a-month salary top players in the commercial sector earned, noted Goh Keng Swee. The next five most senior civil servants received a Mercedes Benz 230.

Return to the Treasury

On 11 August 1970, GEB was back in the Finance Ministry in Fullerton Building. He would be working for an ex-colleague, Hon Sui Sen, who had been persuaded to join politics and was now the Minister for Finance. GEB would have two stints under Hon in the ministry: between 1970 and 1972 and between 1975 and his retirement in 1981. In the intervening period, he was posted to the Foreign Ministry.

Outside the Civil Service, he was remembered for SAFTI and as a formidable intelligence man. Inside, he gained a reputation as an administrator par excellence, quick at making decisions and a straight-talker and -shooter. He was well-known for his wit, which he used to blistering effect whenever he was dissatisfied or annoyed. He made other permanent secretaries nervous.

Former subordinates, to put it frankly, adored him. They found him humorous, even cheeky, and capable of relating to even the lowliest person in the hierarchy despite his own position in the rarefied ranks. A mere encounter or conversation with the tall, big man would leave a deep impression. He was that charismatic. Or rather, his reputation was awe-inspiring.

His portfolio in this first Finance Ministry stint was Economic Development, an obsession of the Singapore government worried about unemployment, economic growth and the loss of Malaysia as a domestic hinterland. The PAP's hopes for a Common Market with Malaysia, which surfaced in pre-merger days, petered out when it was clear that Malaysia was not keen on such a development.

Singapore's economic philosophy had already been set forth earlier by Dr Goh, with the advice of Dutch economist Albert Winsemius. This was to eschew import-substitution in favour of export-led industrialisation, and to court multinational corporations as vehicles to achieve industrial growth. Both themes went against the conventional wisdom of the times, as newly independent countries were wont to display their resilience by being as self-sufficient as possible.

Hon was also chairman of the EDB, in charge of the effort to secure investments. New set-ups the Jurong Town Corporation and the Development Bank of Singapore (DBS) were allocated the roles of providing the industrial infrastructure and industrial financing respectively for the implementation of the new industrialisation programme. By 1972, one-quarter of Singapore's manufacturing firms were either foreign-owned or joint-venture companies, with the United States and Japan as major investors.

When the British announced in 1968 that it would withdraw east of Suez in three years, threatening to grind one-fifth of Singapore's economy to a halt, the Singapore government no longer confined itself to traditional economic pursuits such as improving the infrastructure. Instead, it began to engage in activities that were or could have been the domain of private enterprise. This marked the start of the Civil Service's active involvement in establishing and operating government statutory boards and companies.

The British provided Singapore a soft loan to tide it over for five years. This kitty had to be carefully shepherded. The loan, amounting to £50 million, was agreed to by the British's Defence and Overseas Policy Ministerial Committee. When Singapore needed more than what was given, GEB, as Permanent Secretary for the Finance Ministry, negotiated with the British in May 1971 to increase the aid by another £200,000.

Besides using it to spur British investments and meet the needs of the private sector, $30 million of the aid went into buying taxis, mini-buses and buses to reorganise the public transport system, $18.3 million to purchase heavy equipment for the Jurong Power Station, $4.4 million to build technical training institutes and $3.4 million for a brick factory in Jurong. Almost 83 per cent of the aid would have been spent by 31 March 1972.

GEB was fortunate in a way because he took on his portfolio when the big parameters for Singapore's economic development had already been developed by his predecessors. Far-sighted planning and political stability had more than cushioned any shock from the British withdrawal. The Bases Economic Conversion Department was set up under the Prime Minister's Office to decide what to do with the space, assets and people left in the wake of the British departure.

British bases were converted into commercial use such as shipbuilding and repair, and aerospace and electronic engineering. In 1968, Sembawang Shipyard took over from the Royal Naval Dockyard, while the Singapore Electronic and Engineering replaced the Weapons and Radio Organisation of the same dockyard. Five companies emerged from the takeover of the British Air Force assets. Another group of government enterprises, such as arms-maker Chartered Industries of Singapore, was set up to fill in the security vacuum left by the British.

The dismay and shock of the withdrawal announcement "soon gave way to the perception and utilisation of the not inconsiderable economic opportunities made available with the phased and orderly takeover of the fixed assets and other facilities of the naval, army and air force bases," said Cheng Siok Hwa, writing in the *Southeast Asian Journal of Social Science* in 1979. Dr Cheng was then with the Department of History at Nanyang University.

Running corporations

Wholly-owned and partly-owned industrial and commercial ventures were established either in the name of the "Ministry of Finance Incorporated" a legal entity established in 1959, or through statutory boards such as DBS in which the government owned 49 per cent of the shares, and the International Trading Corporation (INTRACO), where the government stake amounted to 30 per cent. Both DBS and INTRACO were themselves spin-offs of divisions within the EDB.

The government went into the shipbuilding and repairing industry via Jurong, Sembawang and Keppel shipyards. Neptune Orient Lines was incorporated to reduce dependence on foreign-controlled shipping lines. In 1972, Singapore Airlines was brought into being following the break-up of the Malaysia-Singapore Airlines. Singapore Petroleum Company was formed in 1969 to somewhat offset the vast preponderance of foreign companies such as Shell, Esso, British Petroleum and Caltex. The government also formed companies or went into joint ventures in the field of banking, finance and insurance.

As GEB wrote in his 1973 essay on the changes to the Civil Service:

> In economic development, this policy has been implemented by the establishment of industries in direct competition with private enterprise but controlled by Government through the appointment of civil servants on the Boards of Management to ensure that such enterprises are operated viably and do not discriminate against private industry.
>
> The profit motive is still the paramount objective of such industries but the general objective is to keep some control over industries, which for one reason or another would not have been

established but for Government intervention, or because the particular industry is of such importance to the overall economy of Singapore (like shipping, banking, insurance, shipbuilding and oil refining) that some measure of Government intervention is necessary.

GEB presided as a Permanent Secretary during this flurry of unconventional changes in economic structure. Permanent secretaries chaired or sat on these boards, unlike later cohorts who were focused on their ministry's work. In 1971, GEB sat on 11 different boards, including Keppel and Sembawang Shipyards, DBS, INTRACO and Chemical Industries. Sim Kee Boon held ten directorships, Ngiam Tong Dow had seven and J. Y. Pillay sat on six boards, according to a study done by economist Lee Yoke Teng at that time.

If there was one company he was associated with, it would be Keppel Shipyard. GEB took over as a non-executive chairman from Hon in 1970, growing it from shipbuilding and repair work to a diversified conglomerate.

About the same time, a little-known committee called the Directorship and Consultancy Appointments Council, was set up by Hon to not only decide on the civil servants who should be appointed to these companies, but also how they should be rewarded. All remuneration as a result of directorships would be funnelled to the council which would decide every year how much each civil servant-cum-director should be paid for his work in the companies. Sometimes, they got nothing at all and the funds went into the government coffers, according to retired former civil servants. Philip Yeo, who himself chaired several boards, said he took home $1,200 a month in directors' fees, given as a lump sum every year. "It didn't matter how many boards you sat in."

In its initial years, GEB was in this committee, along with a very few senior civil servants. It was the nerve centre of all government-related businesses, and its existence was only hinted at for the first time in the media when the *New Nation* reported in July 1977 that the committee had drawn up new guidelines to ensure government officers do not hold too many company directorships. The council resurfaced in 1985 when then Finance Minister Tony Tan referred to it in Parliament. At that time, *The Straits Times* reported that Tony Tan, Richard Hu, Tan Teck Chwee, Ngiam Tong Dow, J. Y. Pillay, Andrew Chew and Herman Hochstadt were members.

Asked about the operations and composition of the council during his oral history interview, J. Y. Pillay didn't give anything away except to say they met about once a year. Sometimes, he added, younger civil servants with high "current estimated potential" would be posted to the companies if the council thought it would be good for them to gain some business acumen. Pillay told the author that such directorships didn't require much work from civil servants since they were non-executive positions. A Permanent Secretary's main job was to run his ministry well and leave day-to-day operations in the companies to the executives.

The council was disbanded in the mid-1990s to give Temasek Holdings and other government-linked companies the decision-making powers relating to appointments.

On the whole, economists applauded this move to have government involvement in business to spur the growing economy, although they raised questions over whether this was at the expense of developing more entrepreneurs and local businessmen.

GEB himself had a great appreciation of Chinese businessmen in Singapore, which was reinforced over the years. In his oral history recording, he expressed amazement at the quick way businessmen adapted themselves and their businesses to the circumstances. "The Singapore Chinese businessman is a tremendous entrepreneur. During the Japanese Occupation when there were lots of dangers in moving around outside Singapore, it was these people who kept

Singapore kind of fed and clothed through their enterprise," he said. It was a theme he referred to again in a 1984 TV documentary, when he lauded the Chinese businessmen who kept trade going between Singapore and Indonesia even during the Konfrontasi period.

But Chinese business acumen notwithstanding, the government understood that it must wade in where businessmen would fear to tread because of the capital expense or the risk of failure. As GEB said in a radio interview in 1967:

> Here's probably where the public servant or the public manager had a slight edge over the private manager.... It is much easier for him to appreciate the motivation of a national interest than the private manager who has his shareholders who are not strictly interested in nation-building and things like that. Whereas the public manager is accountable to a very definite set of people whose interests are the nation.

The Policy Study Centre that Lee Kuan Yew had set up in 1959 to re-orientate civil servants' mindset from being a colonial apparatus to nation-builder had stopped operating in 1969. With civil servants playing such an immense role in administration and the economy, a Staff Training Institute under the Finance Ministry was set up to equip them with management techniques in 1971.

Public servants going private

By then, economic development had led to a meteoric rise in salaries in the private sector. There was no parallel move in the public sector as the 1959 austerity measures were still in place. The service started facing a brain drain. A 1971 *Straits Times*' survey of 50 senior officers found that 32, all graduates with honours-class degrees, would leave for better pay; only 13 would serve long term in the bureaucracy. The newspaper said that the gap between wages in the government and the private sector had "steadily widened during the past five or six years". Fresh graduates with honours-class degrees could start their careers earning $250 more per month in the private sector; Superscale A officers could earn more than their $3,000 monthly salary in the private sector.

A commission, appointed on 19 April 1966, had recommended the abolition of the Variable Allowance and the incorporation of an amount not exceeding $150 into existing basic salaries. It also advised against introducing new salary scales while recommending higher pay for senior civil servants in the Superscale Grades C to G. These measures were not implemented because the government could not afford to revise the salaries significantly and the private sector was not viewed as a serious competitor for talented personnel, according to political scientist Jon Quah, who specialises in public administration.

In his capacity as Head of Civil Service, GEB lamented the paucity of pay, speaking up at least twice in public. He wanted the salary structure and promotion criteria re-looked. There were too many middle management people doing executive work which could be done by junior clerks. He added that some posts were created to fill promotional needs rather than because of job demands.

A slight reprieve came when the National Wages Council came to being and recommended the Annual Wage Supplement, which started in the Civil Service in 1972. More change came the next year, in 1973, with a revised Civil Service wage structure to bridge the widening gap with private sector salaries. But over the years, civil servants' salaries still continued to lag behind those of their peers in the private sector.

Based on a 1981 Inland Revenue Department survey of more than 30,000 graduates, those in the Civil Service were earning 42 per cent less than their peers in the private sector. So it did not come as a surprise when eight superscale and 67 timescale civil servants left the service for better paying jobs in the private sector. In the following years, the government tried to curb such an outflow by revising the salaries of senior civil servants in 1982, 1988, 1989 and 1994.

Ajith Prasad, who worked for GEB during his second stint at the Finance Ministry, recalled how he and GEB had glimpsed a signboard in their office building, directing people to a promotion exercise for "RK/PS". GEB quipped that he didn't know he was being promoted. When told that RK stood for record keepers and PS was for paper searchers, GEB said that it applied to him: "I am forever keeping records and searching for papers."

GEB never got promoted. In 1979, higher level grades were introduced. The exercise, which led to three senior civil servants' promotion to Staff Grade, was carried out in February 1981, the year GEB was due to retire at the age of 55. He left the service in October.

IX

Making Friends and Influencing Countries

Perhaps it had to do with his experience in dealing with foreign governments. Perhaps it was because the vulnerability of Singapore's position in geopolitics had become so much a part of his work DNA—GEB replaced Stanley Stewart as Permanent Secretary of the Foreign Ministry in December 1972, after just three years at the Finance Ministry. His work at the Special Branch and the Ministry of Interior and Defence had given him a firm grasp of Singapore's security situation, which was an advantage in his new role. Although the direct threat of communism had been eradicated and Singapore was in a better economic situation, the regional outlook was, to put it in weather terms, cloudy with possible thunderstorms.

Even as the Singapore Armed Forces started building up its manpower and hardware, the Singapore Foreign Service was being primed to put the face of a new, independent, sovereign country on the world map. There were plenty of getting-to-know-you visits by top politicians, especially to Afro-Asian countries, and attempts to chalk up allies and memberships in regional and international groups, such as the Non-Aligned Movement. By the time GEB was ensconced in City Hall, there were close to 90 Singaporean foreign service officers posted abroad, including about 25 in ASEAN countries, according to *The Singapore Foreign Service: The First 40 Years* by Gretchen Liu.

The severing of the umbilical cord to the British meant that Singapore needed new friends, while also holding an independent line that was in accord with the national interest. Economically, the Korean and Indochinese wars did the country good. Singapore was a safe haven for keen businessmen who saw opportunities in wartime, whether as a rest and recreation area for American troops or to provide material essential to them.

At the same time, Singapore cast a wary eye on developments up north, remembering how the British had been caught off-guard as Japanese troops made their swift way south in the Second World War. Having decimated communism within its border, it was facing the prospect of new aggression emanating from a communist Indochina, giving effect to the so-called domino theory.

By the time GEB took up his role at the Foreign Ministry, the American effort to block the communist takeover of South Vietnam was on its last legs. GEB must have analysed the prospects with some trepidation. Now that the British colonial masters had pulled out of the country militarily, how was a tiny country going to defend itself and manage its sovereign relations among the great powers of the United States, the Soviet Union and China, who were playing games on the Indochinese chessboard?

The author spoke to Barry Desker, who recalled that after his appointment as assistant secretary (Southeast Asia) in October 1974, his first meeting with GEB was regarding Indochina.

> [GEB] noted that the situation was rapidly turning in a worrying direction with the withdrawal of American forces and congressional pressures for an end to support for the South

Vietnamese regime as well as a likely takeover of Phnom Penh by the Khmer Rouge during their dry season offensive in the months ahead.

Saigon, the capital of South Vietnam, fell in 1975. The communist Khmer Rouge, backed by the Chinese communists, took over Phnom Penh in Cambodia and renamed the country Kampuchea. That same year, the communist Pathet Lao, a Soviet proxy, came to power in Laos.

While GEB was Permanent Secretary during the run-up to such historical events, he wasn't in the ministry long enough to handle the fallout. On 7 July 1975, he went on a seven-week leave. He never returned to the Foreign Ministry and was replaced by Chia Cheong Fook. His short stint, however, was long enough to leave a lasting impression on some foreign service officers at that time. Used to the reserve and reticence of their former boss, Stanley Stewart, they now had a commanding and formidable personality at the helm. As Foreign Minister S. Rajaratnam preferred to deal with conceptual issues, operational matters were left very much to GEB.

Those who had served under him recall his eloquence, lucidity, sense of humour and sometimes unconventional turn of mind. Goh Kian Chee recalled in *The Singapore Foreign Service: The First 40 Years*:

> He had opinions of his own, which he shared with the officers and the minister. He was politically sensitive and had a good sense of our limits and what we could or could not do. He was also a good administrator, had a sense of what the officers were doing and did a number of things that structured MFA a bit better. I think he had a vision of the organisation and how it could grow.

Desker recalled a time when a fellow colleague approached the minister to change a posting and designation that GEB had assigned him. GEB was "furious". The officer got his changed designation, but over a much smaller domain than if he had taken up the first appointment. "For me, it was a lesson in how the old school bureaucrats handled efforts by their staff to use political relationships to push their personal interests instead of following Civil Service norms," he told the author.

Like his father, who was known for his crisp memo-writing in the colonial government, GEB had a concise style of responding to written submissions by the ministry's staff. According to Desker:

> He was known for clear decisions and an unambiguous response handwritten in an easily read neat format. ... He had mastered both the policy issues as well as the administrative aspects. He was able to put across his ideas clearly when he dictated to his secretary, rarely needing to revise a memorandum or letter even on difficult technical issues.

His ability to hold forth at length was legendary. One former subordinate recalled him dictating to his secretary from morning to evening, which resulted in a 30-page report. Other permanent secretaries would have put pen to paper.

GEB was also able to draw on his extensive experience in the Special Branch and Interior and Defence Ministry to rebut arguments from the security agencies which didn't agree with the ministry's line, such as acceding to the Vienna Convention on Consular Relations.

Then there were the tentative steps to engage China, known as ping-pong diplomacy. Informal contacts with China only began in late 1971 following the country's recognition by the United States and its admission to the United Nations. Singapore responded to an invitation to participate in the Afro-Asian Tennis Tournament in Beijing in November 1971. A Chinese table tennis team returned the visit the next year. Other sporting and cultural exchanges followed. This engagement was done against the backdrop of the Chinese Communist Party's (CCP) support for the Malayan Communist Party (MCP) led by Chin Peng.

Back in 1969, Mao Zedong had helped the MCP build a broadcast station in Changsha, Hunan Province. The radio station was named "Voice of Malayan Revolution" and it preached revolution and communism to Singaporeans and Malaysians. The CCP only cut ties with the MCP in the 1980s, which eventually led to the MCP laying down arms and signing the peace agreements in Hat Yai with the Thai and Malaysian governments on 2 December 1989.

GEB must have kept a vigilant eye to ensure China did not interfere in Singapore's domestic politics, even as there was growing rapprochement between the two countries. On 7 October 1974, Foreign Minister S. Rajaratnam and First Chinese Deputy Foreign Minister Qiao Guanhua, who were both in New York to attend the United Nations General Assembly, agreed to begin an exchange of visits by their leaders. Rajaratnam went to Beijing the following March to, among other things, lay the groundwork for Prime Minister Lee Kuan Yew's visit which took place in May 1976.

Closer to home, there were also bridges to mend with Indonesia. In May 1973, Prime Minister Lee Kuan Yew visited Indonesia officially for the first time at the invitation of President Suharto. In Jakarta, they signed a treaty relating to the delimitation of the territorial seas of the two countries in the Strait of Singapore. To mark a break from the Sukarno regime and his policy of Konfrontasi with Malaysia and Singapore, Lee visited the graves of the two Indonesian marines hanged by Singapore on 17 October 1968 for the MacDonald House bombing on 10 March 1965.

Bogaars, who was head of the Special Branch at that time, countering such attacks, was not part of the Singapore delegation. Nor was he involved directly in the next big unexpected event in Singapore: the *Laju* hijacking that took place on 31 January 1974. Two Japanese and two Arabs had hijacked a ferryboat, taking five crewmen hostage after they had failed to blow up the Shell oil refinery on Pulau Bukom.

The lead agencies were the Ministry of Home Affairs and the Security and Intelligence Department. GEB had to handle the diplomatic front. The role of the Foreign Ministry was to maintain contact with the Japanese and North Korean embassies and Arab government. In the book *The Singapore Foreign Service: The First 40 Years,* Tan Boon Seng, See Chak Mun and Lee Chiong Giam were named as the foreign service officers who worked under his direction on this matter.

Although foreign relations tend to be macro in nature, GEB made time to sort out the smaller details affecting his staff. In his memoirs *Glimpses and Reflections,* the late President Wee Kim Wee recounted the time when he was appointed Singapore High Commissioner to Malaysia in 1973. To suit up for the part, he had a clothing allowance of $400, which was only enough for a tailored lounge suit and an extra pair of trousers. He had to cough up another $1,200 for a tuxedo, dress shirt, bow tie and morning suit from Melwani's in the Arcade at Raffles Place. There was no allowance for his wife. His "mild" protest to a foreign service officer fell on deaf ears—until GEB made a trip up to Kuala Lumpur a few months later. "I raised the issue with him. He was taken aback and asked if I had the receipts from Melwani's. I had. When he returned to Singapore, I was suitably reimbursed."

Writing in his memoirs *From Estate to Embassy,* former diplomat K. Kesavapany wrote of how, as a young foreign service officer, he had qualms about being posted to Malaysia as Singapore's Deputy High Commissioner in 1972. The ex-Malaysian had left the country less than five years ago and was worried about how he would be received in Malaysia. GEB agreed with him about his concerns—and he was posted to the Singapore embassy in Indonesia.

GEB had a more lasting influence on Raymond Wong, who, among the various posts he held, was Singapore's ambassador to South Korea from 1990 to 1994. In *The Little Red Dot: Reflections by Singapore's Diplomats*, he recalled how he tried to move from the Finance to Foreign Ministry by applying for a post there and was hauled up for not going through the proper transfer process. He thought that was the end of the episode until he was summoned to see GEB, the Permanent Secretary of the ministry he hoped to transfer to.

> It turned out to be an interesting interview that changed the course of my Civil Service career. I still remember to this day the kind advice he gave me. He mused that the young think that they know everything, but real wisdom would come only with age and long experience. He was right of course. I remain grateful to him for giving me the chance to join the Foreign Service.

Another diplomat who stayed the course because of GEB was Kishore Mahbubani. He recalled how, after just a few years in the service, he had wanted to quit when he qualified for an overseas scholarship to do a master's degree in philosophy. He reckoned that the bureaucracy would not agree to let him go on leave nor approve of his choice of study. "I was sure it wouldn't be supported by MFA. In any case, I would have to cut through reams of red tape to get approval."

After he had tendered his resignation letter, the young Mahbubani was called into GEB's office. It was his first meeting with GEB. "He said I don't have to quit, just take no-pay leave. He made arrangements for some payment so I didn't have to worry about supporting my mother at home. ... That's why I stayed on."

Mahbubani retired from MFA in 2004.

X

Controller of the Purse

On 8 July 1975, *The Straits Times* ran a front-page story that took civil servants by surprise. The headline said: "Howe is new head of the Civil Service. Bogaars to take on another post." Besides stating that Howe Yoong Chong, then chairman and general manager of the PSA, would be the new chief, the newspaper also reported that Chia Cheong Fook, a director in the Defence Ministry, was replacing GEB as Permanent Secretary of the Foreign Ministry. It added cryptically that GEB had gone on leave the previous day for "personal reasons" but would "take up another appointment shortly".

Staff at the Finance Ministry's Budget Division also learnt that their Permanent Secretary, Tan Chok Kian, had been moved to the Social Affairs Ministry and that, for the time being, J. Y. Pillay, who was Permanent Secretary of the Revenue Division, would be overseeing the Budget Division as well.

There was considerable speculation about the "personal reasons" and whether they led to GEB having to relinquish his postings. Word that it had to do with his personal indiscretions that had upset his wife and the political leadership made the rounds. The talk then was that he would be taking some form of early retirement; he was 49.

On 25 August 1975, after an unusually long seven-week leave, GEB re-surfaced at the helm of the Finance Ministry, back with his old boss, Hon Sui Sen. While he was in charge of Economic Development in his earlier stint, he was now in charge of the Budget Division.

The ministry was a top-heavy one. Besides Pillay, there were Ngiam Tong Dow (Development) and Sim Kee Boon, who was heading a cross-ministry Economic Activation Committee, dealing with measures to address the economic challenges following the global oil crises of the 1970s.

Within days, GEB called a meeting of senior officers. The most senior staff took the front row of seats around the conference table, while subordinates lined the walls. For the officers, it was a surprise to be called to such a meeting with their top boss, as previous permanent secretaries interacted mainly with their immediate deputies. GEB started talking about the importance of Treasury work through the ages and the high esteem accorded to Treasury officials the world over, including at the Imperial Courts in China and that of Emperor Napoleon in France. They would be ferried in palanquins and on sedan chairs, he quipped.

He then highlighted what he thought Budget Division's work priorities should be—revamping the processes for evaluating and funding the government's operating and capital costs. After fielding a few questions from the senior staffers seated around the conference table, he turned to the others seated just behind them and asked: "What do the people in the cheap seats have to say?"

That was the first taste they got of his humour. And they remembered it well enough to explore hiring a "sedan chair" to seat GEB and to carry him to his car at the end of the retirement dinner they had organised for him at the Hilton Hotel in 1981. As a sedan chair was not available, they made do with an ordinary hotel dining chair.

GEB had a way of putting people at ease, chatting to all and sundry. Unlike other senior civil servants, he did not keep a distance from his subordinates. It was this quality that endeared him to his subordinates, who were not only in awe of him, but also remember to this day the voluble and garrulous man who tickled them with his jokes.

In the ministry, GEB gave the highest priority to revamping the budget process, which had come in for some criticism in Parliament earlier that year. He was of the view that the answer to these criticisms was to replace the "line-item" expenditure budget system that had been in place since the colonial days with a more modern "programme and performance budgeting system", like that used by many state and local governments in developed countries. He had first advocated this change way back in 1960 when he was MOF's deputy secretary in charge of the Budget. But he had spent too little time there to effect change because he was posted to the Special Branch soon after. The status quo remained.

During the 1975 Budget debate, the budget system came under scathing criticism from Tan Eng Liang, MP for River Valley and later Senior Minister of State for National Development. Tan told Parliament that the Finance Ministry's Budget officers often failed to consult departments to clarify their proposals and were arbitrary in their decisions.

The parliamentary Estimates Committee set up to study the problems with the budget process recommended that each ministry submit, together with its annual budget proposal, a performance review analysing its major achievements against previous targets and relating its budget proposals with the corresponding targets for the new financial year. Such performance reviews would link budget requirements with the work plans of ministries, providing a more objective basis for budget decisions.

When GEB came on board, he personally drafted a sample of such a review for the Labour Ministry, drawing on data in the ministry's most recent annual report, budget estimates and other sources, recalled Ajith Prasad, who was involved in the revamp then. This served as a template for budget officers to adapt for their respective ministries. In short, GEB illustrated how a budget request, instead of merely listing the "things to be bought", could be linked to "things to be achieved".

The new system became operational in 1978 and was further refined under successive permanent secretaries. It was a more complex venture for finance officers in the various ministries, who now had to identify performance indicators and write analytical essays to accompany their request for funds. This was in the days of "hard copy" with no Internet searches to locate information nor spreadsheets to simplify computations. It led to some moaning among finance staff, recalled Prasad. One ministry even ignored requests for performance indicators but had to do so after the lapse was raised at a Cabinet meeting.

GEB brought in word processors, which was a great advance on the days when everything was done on typewriters. Herman Hochstadt, who succeeded GEB as Permanent Secretary, wrote in his memoirs, *lives & times of hrh*: "When I was there, we tried to simplify even further by having the linkage so that the word processors will be communicating with each other throughout the system."

Biting witticisms and curbing demands

The Budget Review meeting following the annual call for budget proposals was the biggest exercise for the department. This was when

GEB's insights and sharp wit were on full display. His subordinates loved how he rattled the cages of senior civil servants who had not thought through their requests for a bigger budget. He had a wicked way of teasing people which left them deflated or flummoxed.

Ex-subordinates have a string of incidents stored in their memories of senior civil servants caught on the backfoot. For example, he told officers in charge of parks who wanted a budget for grass-cutting on a nationwide basis that they should rear goats which would eat the grass as well as give milk.

In response to a claim by the Public Works Department (PWD) that it was "absurd" that it had only been provided with three staffers when it had divided the island into four regions for building maintenance purposes, he said that it was even more absurd that the PWD had gone ahead to set up four regions when only three positions had been authorised.

National Development ministry officials were flabbergasted at his response to their proposal for a budget for research on pig waste management to minimise pollution problems. He told them that they had got it wrong. The most effective solution, he said with a straight face, was to breed a constipated pig.

Ex-colleagues insisted that GEB was not being churlish nor dismissive. He enjoyed keeping civil servants on their toes. Seah Kia Ger, who was now with the ministry's Budget Division, said it was GEB's way of releasing tension in the room, and to make sure that civil servants knew that there must be priorities for the purse.

"I have only seen him lose his temper once, when a department head from the Home Affairs Ministry kept on pressing him to say yes. He said: 'This is enough for you and if it's not enough, go back and tell your minister who can appeal to my minister.'" The department head stormed out of the room, but nothing further was heard on this.

Perhaps he realised that it was unlikely that his minister would want to pick a fight with the formidable GEB.

Another civil servant who was stymied by GEB was Cham Tao Soon, the first president of the Nanyang Technological University (formerly the Nanyang Technical Institute). Writing in his book, *Life at Speed*, he recalled how his first encounter with GEB was "not a pleasant one". In 1981, "I had to see him regarding funding for NTI. He was not sympathetic to my desire to put NTI on par with NUS." Cham had to go to the Education Minister Tony Tan to resolve the issue. Dr Tan consulted the Finance Minister Hon Sui Sen, who said that he had to go along with his Permanent Secretary's views. "Finally, Dr Tan had to appeal to the PM, who eventually overruled the MOF."

Low Sin Leng recalled in *Pioneers Once More* what GEB said when she appeared with permanent secretaries Goh Kim Leong (Education) and Philip Yeo (Defence) to ask for a budget for computers: "We walked into the room, Bogaars sitting at the end. He said, 'Oh, I see that you have very important supporters with you.'"

Recalling the incident, Yeo told the author that GEB gave Goh Kim Leong a good scolding for not settling the paperwork for the $2 million system. That was when Yeo told GEB that the system was already up and running and the money was actually owed to him. "So I told him, Mr Bogaars, you can scold him but I'm the one not being paid." Yeo said he had done as Goh Keng Swee ordered: set up a computer in the Education Ministry which Dr Goh had taken over. "There was no memo, no nothing. We just did it. Mr Bogaars laughed and said okay. That generation, Howe Yoon Chong, Dr Goh, George Bogaars, they can decide. Now people need to know how to write a memo. That generation is gone."

Prasad recalled how GEB denied a police request for a budget of several million dollars to set up and replace their eight land division headquarters, and to add four more on the island. "It didn't fit his concept of effective policing. He thought they shouldn't be hiding in air-con comfort but out on the ground to know what's happening." GEB advocated reducing the number of HQ stations but complementing these with smaller neighbourhood police posts from which the police could mount their patrols. This approach was eventually adopted.

In contrast, he was more than amenable to a police request for more marine boats to guard the coastline in the aftermath of the *Laju* ferry hijacking when foreign saboteurs got onto the island unseen. He got experts from Keppel Shipyard, where he was chairman, to help the police review their planning parameters and come up with numbers that could be justified on the basis of affordability and security. "He knew how to make use of his network," said Prasad.

One example of his decision-making came from GEB himself, in an interview with the *Management Development* newsletter in 1981. He had read complaints about the low quality of local productions by the then Singapore Broadcasting Corporation, forerunner of Mediacorp. He admitted to rejecting a $7 million proposal to build bigger studios to raise the quality of local TV productions.

> I was against it because I thought people had not really understood the problem. The problem is not just to spend lots of money getting XYZ who can do a bit of acting to come along and act out a script which someone else has written.
>
> If you are talking about local production of TV films, it means a different kind of thing. It means you are going to start somewhere and must end up very much higher than it is now and not only showing to your own people but exporting them, selling them, and then if you look at the other countries that are doing it—Australia, India, Indonesia, Hong Kong, Taiwan—you then say, how do they do this and why do they do this?
>
> And one thread that runs through all of them, I may be wrong, is all of them have film industries. They have the career opportunities for people to act, to put up props, because there is a place where they can earn a living.

He didn't think there was an industry to sustain the people required to produce films. "The fellow goes to the studio, goes home, goes back, all in his spare-time. In the day-time he may be working as an office boy. ... Very good artistes are not going to be here in Singapore acting for your films. They are going to earn thousands of dollars elsewhere."

Apart from his work on the budget process, another lasting influence was his initiative to have "morning coffee" with his staff. This was held every morning for a set period in the staff lounge for administrative officers to talk shop or otherwise. Dileep Nair described it as a "majlis" to talk about anything and everything, including gossip about so and so. "It was great for newbies because they can interact closely with the man."

Said Sim Cheng Tee in his oral history records: "He felt that we should all get together away from our desks and exchange knowledge, exchange views [and] opinions amongst ourselves as admin officers. It was through a subscription basis—all of us paid something towards the cost of the coffee."

Seah Kia Ger described the coffee club as a way to learn to see the bigger picture during the budgeting process.

> Once, he said we should discuss the plan to build recreational facilities on a piece of land in Pasir Ris. We ended up discussing how this would fit in at a time when we were still upgrading hospitals and deciding whether to have an MRT in Singapore. It was about priorities. We didn't have much money then. Every cent had to count.

This coffee club survives till today as the Treasury Coffee Club, with mainly ex-Finance Ministry officials. They meet regularly for lunch to talk about old times and keep up with each other. GEB was a guest at a couple of their get-togethers, including a Christmas party in 1986.

GEB didn't seem to mind retiring from the Civil Service. In fact, he was looking forward to more free time as the part-time chairman of Keppel as well as of the National Iron and Steel Mill. He told his daughters that he would spend five mornings at Keppel and two afternoons at NatSteel every week.

He wrote: "The pay is very good and is more than I am getting in the civil service excluding my pension (which is tax-free). So we should be able to live in relative comfort for the next three years."

He could not have foreseen what a troubled three years he would have.

GEB with his parents on his graduation day, 26 July 1952.

GEB and
Dorothy's
wedding day. *Left
to right*: GEB's
mother, Tom
Hart, Dorothy,
GEB, Mrs Hart
and GEB's father.

GEB and Christina,
approx. 1964.

Christina, Dorothy and GEB.

Dorothy and GEB's
pomeranian, Penhurst
Campbell who was also
known as Prinsz.

GEB attending the hoisting of the new Singapore navy flag at Telok Ayer Basin in his capacity as Permanent Secretary (Ministry of Interior and Defence), 5 May 1967. Credit: Ministry of Information and the Arts Collection, courtesy of National Archives of Singapore.

GEB attending a function with Goh Keng Swee (*second from left*) and Kirpa Ram Vij (*far right*), likely during GEB's defence days.

GEB (*centre*) with Percy Pennefather (*on GEB's right*). Pennefather was the assistant commissioner of police and Head of the Internal Security Department.

GEB's work desk, likely at the Fullerton Building.

A clock presented to GEB by his Budget Division staff.

GEB at the signing of the Keppel Shipyard Guaranteed Bonds Agreement, 1982.

GEB and his family in hospital after GEB's first heart attack. *Left to right*: Michael, Christina, GEB, Dorothy and Paulina.

GEB in hospital with some hospital physiotherapy staff after he suffered a stroke.

XI

In a Storm over Keppel

As a postgraduate student, George Edwin Bogaars wrote about the history and development of Tanjong Pagar Dock Company for his master's thesis. In 1970, he was appointed chairman of Keppel Shipyard, which encompassed the dockyard. It was no longer an academic exercise. While his thesis was focused on the genesis, initial years and growth of the dockyard, he now had the task of making the company it had morphed into a going concern. Today's Keppel Corporation bears little resemblance to its original incarnation in the 19th century as two small ship-repair companies which moved into the hands of the British authorities. These dockyards and operations later came under the Singapore Harbour Board, predecessor of the PSA (Port Singapore Authority).

As part of Singapore's industrialisation exercise, Keppel Shipyard was incorporated in September 1968, under the ownership of the Ministry of Finance, to take over operations and control of assets that were worth about $100 million. They consisted of four docks at Keppel Harbour, two docks at Tanjong Pagar and one slipway at Tanjong Rhu. In the 1960s, Singapore had yet to establish itself as a ship-repair centre in the world shipping community. But official projections showed that there was room to grow from the current contribution of $70 million a year, or two per cent of the country's gross domestic product, to about $500 million a year by the 1970s.

Keppel's first chairman was Hon Sui Sen, the head of the EDB who had to quit the post two years later when he became a politician and was appointed the Finance Minister. Although there were other pioneer directors on the board, GEB was picked from the Civil Service to replace Hon as the non-executive chairman. At that time, he was Permanent Secretary of the Finance Ministry and Head of Civil Service. It bears noting that very few men were at the helm of Singapore's government-driven industrialisation in those days. It was a closed circle of senior civil servants, rotated on boards to expose them to the world of business while still making sure the companies served both corporate and national interests. They were viewed as "trusted men" handpicked by the Directorship and Consultancy Appointments Council, which reported to the prime minister.

The newly incorporated Keppel Shipyard remained under old management, the British Swan Hunter group, for a contracted period of four years. By the time GEB took the helm, he had an almost all-local management crew of 30-somethings. A naval architect, Chua Chor Teck, was managing director and an accountant, Tay Kim Kah, became financial controller. They were his left and right hands, the prime movers of Keppel Shipyard and who also took the fall when the company later made what was then viewed as a bad buy—the purchase of Straits Steamship in 1983.

Tay Kim Kah noted that it was now almost universally acknowledged that the buy, then the largest corporate takeover at more than $400 million, was a good one as it gave Keppel a foothold in the property arena. "George was a bold man. A visionary. He was willing to take a risk and willing to trust his executives to manage the company even though we were just young punks," he told the author.

Ang Kong Hua, now chairman of SembCorp, concurred. Ang was managing director of the then National Iron and Steel Mills when GEB became its chairman in 1984. He told of how GEB had encouraged him to go ahead and invest in a solar energy project, saying, "This is precisely the sort of industry that NatSteel and Singapore should get involved with!"

> So, I took it to the board and we proceeded with Singapore's first solar panel manufacturing plant. Alas, we were several decades too early, and the plant eventually shuttered. However, that was the beginning of a long period of technology investments and corporate transformation at NatSteel that created over $5 billion of shareholder value over the next 25 years.

Risk taker

One early risk GEB took with Keppel was buying into a family-owned company known as Far East Shipbuilding in 1971. He told *The Business Times* in an interview on 20 July 1983: "The opportunity came to us through a board member. He indicated that there was a big block of shares which was being 'shopped' around and suggested that Keppel should buy it as an investment. This investment marked the beginning of our diversification."

The board member was Tay, who had heard from a broker that the company was looking for a buyer. Although it would be just a 13 per cent stake, GEB was sure that the private owners would come asking for more money because it had a contract to build oil rigs with Levingston Shipyard based in the United States. He knew they did not have enough working capital. GEB liked that the company was venturing into oil rigs, expanding into new but related products. He was right. Soon enough, the owners came a-begging and Keppel increased its stake to 39 per cent. Tay recalled spending less than half a million dollars in all.

GEB sent a Keppel man to run operations: Loh Wing Siew, then Keppel's executive director and general manager. The company later became a fully owned subsidiary, Far East Levingston, now known as Keppel FELS. Loh told Colin Cheong, author of *Can Do!: The Spirit of Keppel FELS*, that he initially said no to his chairman when he was asked to go to FELS. "I knew nothing about the offshore business. I eventually said 'yes' because Bogaars was very persuasive. I also knew that this was one of our first major subsidiaries and we had to run it well."

Clearly, GEB had already started thinking of spreading Keppel's interests in its early years, given that the shipping industry was cyclical by nature with peaks and troughs. Keppel couldn't survive on only ship-repair work. Some other business would have to make up for the expected declines in revenue from ship repair and shipbuilding. It built barges at first and later, when the docks were upgraded, went into constructing mini bulk carriers. It also started ship "conversions", such as turning tankers into drill ships and sheep carriers.

One project which Keppel would rather erase from its corporate history is the drill-ship *Eniwetok*, which was converted from a bulk ore carrier. The completion of its conversion was announced with much fanfare in December 1982. On 29 January 1983, the tall mast of the drill-ship snagged a cable stretching between the mainland and Sentosa. Two cable cars plunged into the sea and seven passengers were killed. The inquiry that followed put the blame mainly on the master and pilot of the vessel, who did not ascertain the actual height of the ship.

Expanding abroad

The ship repair and shipbuilding industry was a labour intensive one. By the early 1970s, Singapore was facing a manpower crunch in a market of increasingly higher wages. Generous pay increases, averaging ten per cent annually between 1979 and 1985, were handed out in keeping with official recommendation. There was also greater competition from South Korea and China with their bigger pool of cheap labour.

In 1974, GEB led a delegation to the Philippines to promote investment in ASEAN. He was then Permanent Secretary of the Foreign Ministry. The setting up of a yard in Batangas, about two and a half hours by car away from Manila, was proposed. Choo Chiau Beng, now rector of Residential College Four at the National University of Singapore, recalled muddling through the bureaucratic maze before a plot of padi fields was settled upon. The next year, Keppel put down roots in Batangas, building a shipyard from scratch, the first Singapore company to venture into an ASEAN country. Like he did with Loh, GEB plunged Choo, who joined the organisation in 1971, into the Philippines to oversee its start-up. At that time, Choo was a naval architect and director at Singapore Slipway. Tay said that this was GEB's way of nurturing talent and making them stay with the company. "A shipyard in Singapore would be way too small for someone like Chiau Beng. So Bogaars always made sure the best people had bigger jobs that they would have their imprints on, so that they would stay with the company."

GEB would say in an interview with the *Management Development* newsletter about leadership that he was never comfortable about hiring only high-fliers. "You want only a couple of chiefs. The others just run round scalping the pale faces. One chief is enough. You don't want too many fellows smoking peace pipes." The way to build the chief was to make sure there was a consensus that he was a cut above the rest and plunge him into jobs that can showcase his mettle.

Choo stayed in the Philippines for four years before he was asked to return to help Loh Wing Siew with the management of Keppel FELS.

Over the years, Keppel Philippines went on to buy three other shipyards including in Cebu and Subic Bay, becoming the dominant player in the country, repairing, building and converting ships, as well as constructing offshore structures such as oil rigs. In 1987, it made a record of 18 million pesos ($1.8 million) of profit, on a turnover of 68.3 million pesos.

Keppel's ventures in Thailand and Malaysia, however, didn't pan out and the company pulled out quickly. It was the nature of business that not all projects would succeed, said Tay, adding that GEB did not put the blame on anyone. GEB was only concerned about Keppel's prospects in the long-run, not the immediate term. He was convinced Keppel would be strong enough to weather small storms, Tay said.

By the mid-1970s, Singapore had gained a reputation as a major international ship-repair centre, particularly for large vessels. From 1966 to 1974, the number of establishments for ship repair and shipbuilding increased from 26 to 50; the numbers of employed from 9,200 to 32,000, which was 11 per cent of the industrial workforce as of 1975. Revenue also increased from $80 million to $720 million. Revenue increased by 30 per cent over the year (from 1974 to 1975) with a 25 per cent increase in the building of ships and oil rigs, and a 60 per cent increase in ship-repairing.

Keppel's business methods were not always orthodox, and the way it was operating at the "borderline", as Tay put it, probably raised a few eyebrows. In the early days of Singapore's industrialisation, with so much of the financial infrastructure still in its nascent stages, it seemed that the pioneers were pretty savvy at finding ways round roadblocks.

Keppel wanted to get into finance but didn't have the financial muscle to buy stakes in a bank. So it operated a credit company which was later given a licence to become a full-fledged finance company known in its early days as Shing Loong Finance. That wasn't enough for Keppel's ambitions: it wanted to start a bank. It decided to incorporate K Bank in the Cayman Islands, just as the Bank of America did. It didn't succeed in getting an offshore banking licence from the Singapore authorities but the opportunity came in the late 1970s when it bought a ten per cent stake in the Asia Commercial Bank. This later became the Keppel TatLee Bank, until it was sold off to OCBC in August 2001.

Tay said that Keppel had been diversifying so rapidly that he himself sat on more than 70 boards of Keppel's subsidiaries. In 1975, Keppel became the first company outside Japan to issue an Asian Currency Bond unit. In 1980, Keppel Shipyard was listed on the Singapore Stock Exchange. Thirty million ordinary shares were issued, at $3.30 per share. It raised $99 million.

The Straits Steamship buy

Then came the biggest risk of all: moving into property. GEB had set out the direction in Keppel's 1980 annual report: "The Keppel Group's involvement in property development is still small. There are plans to expand further and a major project is now in the pipeline."

Tay said that Keppel had been looking to enter the property business but didn't have much luck finding a foothold. All it had at that time were a few bungalows for the staff's recreational use. Then came talk that the British-based Ocean Transport and Trading was looking to offload Straits Steamship, which operated a series of coastal vessels and was engaged in oilfield and engineering activities. GEB, Chua and Tay started discussions on a buy-out with the owners. They weren't interested in the marine side of the company, but in its prime property assets. Straits Steamship, a listed company, owned Ocean Building, Bukit Timah Plaza, Keppel House and a Cluny Hill estate.

The executives worked out the numbers, met the owners in London and brought the deal to the board of directors. It would cost the company $408 million, around 70 per cent of its capital. It was a huge bet. In fact, it was betting the shop.

In his oral history records, Professor Bernard Tan, who was sitting on the board at the time, recalled how the news was broken:

> I always remember the board meeting where he announced that Keppel is going to buy Straits Steamship. He looked at Tay Kim Kah who was then the director of finance at Keppel, and asked Kim Kah, "Shall we tell them about project S?" This is the project. So he announced to us that he bought Straits Steamship and to tell you the truth, Straits Steamship was not viewed as a good purchase because it used up all of Keppel's reserves and the corporate culture of Keppel and Straits Steamship is completely different.

There was some consternation at the size of the takeover, the biggest in Singapore at that time. While some hailed it as a coup, questions were asked about whether this had official sanction from the Finance Ministry or was merely a private decision made by a few people. Did, for example, the Directorship and Consultancy Appointments Council know of the buy?

Tay said: "I was told that it was raised at a Cabinet meeting that the management acted without prior authorisation and that the price was excessive. I was also told that Mr Hon affirmed his prior knowledge and approval of our actions."

J. Y. Pillay, now Rector of the College of Alice and Peter Tan at NUS, who sat on the council then, said it was not the practice of the council to intervene in the investment decisions of government-linked companies. Both Pillay and Ang said that the company chairman was the prime decision maker. In the days before the financial industry took off with fund managers and analysts probing into corporate affairs, the board of directors only had to deal with retail investors, many of whom could not be bothered to turn up for annual general meetings.

Asked about the control over diversification of government companies by MP for Jalan Kayu, Hwang Soo Jin, Tony Tan, the Finance Minister at that time, said in Parliament: "It would, however, not be desirable, in my view, to hobble government companies to such an extent that the managements are inhibited from making normal commercial decisions without reference to the Ministry of Finance."

In the case of Straits Steamship, there was the added worry about the deal being done in cash, rather than shares, which meant interest payments would put pressure on its soon-to-be depleted reserves. For a company dependent on revenues in an industry which was trending downwards, it looked like a dangerous place to be.

When the deal was closed in November 1983, more rumblings were heard, both in corporate and political circles. Keppel had purchased 58 per cent of Straits Steamship at $1.98 per share from UK-based Ocean Transport and Trading, which was said to be too high a price by the time the deal was done. Rumblings became louder when Straits Steamship reported a heavy interim loss in the first half of 1984, incurring pre-tax losses of $6.63 million against pre-tax profits of $2.68 million in the same period the previous year.

In an interview with *The Singapore Monitor* on 16 June 1985, Bogaars said he had not been told to expect such poor numbers from Straits Steamship. He brushed away suggestions that his managers might not have been diligent enough. "It doesn't mean that the company is no good. It just means that the company has run into a bad patch. We went in and cleaned up as best as we could," he said.

You've got to look at this thing impartially. It's one company taking over another, it's done all the time. In fact, far bigger deals take place. All the reasons for the takeover were sound reasons. Straits will contribute to Keppel's welfare in time to come because it's a solid company with very good assets.

He also said that Keppel was not the only interested buyer at that time. A distinguished Singapore businessman, whom he did not name, had also expressed interest. "If everyone thought that Straits was that bad, why was such a highly reputable businessman offering to buy it? So it must be a question of price that annoyed whoever it annoyed." It was an oblique way of saying that someone else who had his hopes of buying the company extinguished then started to bad-mouth the buy.

Speaking to the author, Tay was dismissive of the market analyses. He took issue especially with statements that Keppel racked up a $845 million debt at the end of 1983 because it paid too high a price for Straits Steamship. Stories that it was floundering or in crisis were exaggerated, he added. Tay gave some numbers: The debt due to the $408 acquisition was only $114 million. The rest of the debt was due to its own operations. Keppel had assets and it could still borrow or raise money if it needed to. In June 1984, for example, two months after GEB left Keppel, the company raised $156 million of capital through a rights issue.

The conventional wisdom some years later is that Keppel made a good buy, but did so at the wrong time. The global offshore and marine industry was going downhill then. In 1981, total turnover rose by 43 per cent to pass the three-quarter-billion-dollar mark, while pre-tax profits shot up by 47 per cent to an all-time high of $153 million.

The next year, the slowdown started to bite. Turnover declined to $645 million. Pre-tax profits, however, rose to $160 million, because its offshore division, namely Far East Levingston, was doing well. In 1983, pre-tax profit plunged to just $28 million. The next year, it was down to $5.4 million.

Tay said. "I would stress that management was aware of the impending downturn. The opportunity for Keppel to diversify into property development outweighed this concern. Keppel had previously encountered a number of business downturns without a scar. There was no reason to suspect the impending downturn would cripple Keppel." For example, despite the oil crisis in the 1970s, Keppel remained relatively unscathed with $40 million in pre-tax profits yearly except in 1978, when it closed the year with just $6 million.

Even Keppel FELS didn't have an easy start. Choo Chiau Beng, who was sent there after four years in the Philippines, recalled the mess in 1978. "Every project was late; every project was losing money because their cost control was really poor. After the job is finished, the rig leaves the yard, they still haven't paid the subcontractors and suppliers," he told the author. Much work had to be put into merging the bureaucratic structure of the American cowboy-run business and the can-do spirit of the Keppel folks.

In other words, Keppel's management remained supremely confident that the company would come out ahead in a few years despite its hefty purchase of Straits Steamship.

It did. But not before GEB was replaced as chairman.

Good deal or botched buy?

Hindsight, as they say, is perfect. GEB took a risk with the Straits Steamship buy because he was convinced that moving into property would lift the company's fortunes in the long term. Ang Kong Hua thinks the bold move to raid Keppel's reserves was unsettling to many. Most boards prefer to take modest stakes or go into a joint venture in case the project doesn't pan out. Asked if he thought GEB was too much of a visionary and less of a details man, he said that even if this was so, his executives were first-class men who knew their numbers. "George Bogaars had gumption. And he had good managers. First-class men," he told the author.

Choo Chiau Beng thought that Keppel should not have used its cash hoard to place the bet, as orders for ship repairs were already slowing down, leading to dwindling revenues. One bank, he told the author, had pulled its credit lines because of talk that Keppel was in financial straits.

Cham Tao Soon, a Keppel director at that time, said in his book that GEB became chairman "at a difficult time". He said: "Some of the things he did, I would not fault him for. In a large business, you have to take certain risks. Otherwise, you would not grow."

Although GEB retired from the Civil Service in 1981, his chairmanship at Keppel was extended for another three years, to April 1984. That was when word was sent down that he would be replaced by Sim Kee Boon, Head of Civil Service at that time. Tay Kim Kah resigned soon after and left for Hong Kong to find work. Tay said that Chua Chor Teck wanted to quit too but was persuaded to stay on for at least a year. Unfortunately, Chua contracted liver cancer and died in 1986 at the age of 46.

Another casualty was the merchant bank Jardine Fleming, which was faulted by the Monetary Authority of Singapore (MAS) for giving Keppel bad advice on the buy. Its argument that its role was peripheral was swept away. Tay said the bank was correct to say that it wasn't in a position to advise on the buy. It was already a done deal by the time the bank came on board. Jardine Fleming was told to advise shareholders on whether the price was satisfactory. But this was not the only issue MAS faulted Jardine for. In 1982, Jardine also gave poor advice to the minority shareholders of Singapore Land

Limited in recommending a rights issue in which the proceeds were to finance the purchase of five cargo vessels. Its banking licence was revoked.

Keppel's financial "faux pas" had been preceded by the cable car tragedy. Keppel was admonished too, by the Commission of Inquiry, for breaching its common law duty of care for its neighbours. The results were released to the public on 15 January 1984. During the inquiry, the PSA recommended a height ban of 45 metres, which would have put Keppel in a quandary as almost half of its ships berthed at Keppel's Oil Wharf were big container vessels of at least 46 metres tall.

In the Committee of Inquiry report, Keppel had a terse statement:

> Keppel Shipyard is of the belief that the only criterion to consider is the financial and economic one. Politics and attractions for tourists should not weigh with the commission when balanced against the earning powers of the cable car system and the loss to Keppel in business if they are to limit themselves to working on vessels of 52 metres in height or less.
>
> The commission will have to seriously consider whether it is economically more important to keep Keppel Shipyard earning as it does, or the cable car system which, in Keppel Shipyard's submission, is really only a tourist attraction. On balance, if it is to be a question of limiting Keppel Shipyard as to make it no longer viable or competitive with other shipyards in Singapore, then it is obvious which has to go.

The issue was later resolved by designating the waterway around Keppel Harbour as a Height Restriction Area, vessels taller than 52 metres were banned from the area, while those between 48 and 52 metres had to seek the written approval of the port master to enter, shift in or leave the area. In 1986, the PSA also installed a laser system to detect the height of ships entering the restricted area. Alarms would go off at the Port Operations Centre when vessels exceeding the programmed heights crossed the laser beam.

Keppel's response couldn't have made many people happy, especially the doyens in charge of the cable car system and the development of Sentosa. Ngiam Tong Dow was chairman of the Sentosa Development Corporation then. Howe Yoon Chong was the Chairman of Singapore Cable Car Pte Ltd.

A *Singapore Monitor* article on 25 April 1984 said that GEB wished to stay on the board for two more years to justify the takeover of Straits Steamship. He was convinced that Keppel could easily turn around Straits Steamship, just as it did with Far East Levingston. The marine industry was cyclical in nature and property prices would not remain depressed for too long in a developing Singapore. He said this would "vindicate" Finance Minister Hon Sui Sen's trust in him and Keppel. Hon had died in office in October 1983, at the age of 67. "He believed the Straits acquisition was the right thing. He was prepared to stop any attempts to abort it. I would have given anything to prove his trust," GEB was reported saying.

> Some of the weaknesses resulting in the losses can be remedied. The consolidation of Keppel companies that we have acquired up to now can be resolved. The core business—the marine industry—won't be as bad as last year [1983] but observers cannot see much pick-up.
>
> I would have wanted to stay on for two more years. I would have been able to advise on matters such as competition with neighbouring countries with lower costs in the shipbuilding and ship repairing business. We can turn Straits around in two years. Mr Sim Kee Boon is of the same view.

While Sim Kee Boon pruned some parts of Keppel, like selling off the vessels belonging to Straits Steamship, this is not to say that GEB and the old management would not have done the same. Tay said that just by sitting on their hands, Keppel would have righted itself and come out ahead. In 1986, Keppel's fortunes turned when it was back in the black with a pre-tax profit of $7.3 million, against a loss of $49.9 million the previous year.

GEB's removal was seen by many as a fall from grace. But there were signs earlier that he was headed for the wilderness when he had to relinquish his position as Head of Civil Service in July 1975 to Howe Yoon Chong, who was then the chairman and general manager of the PSA. Prime Minister Lee Kuan Yew himself was said to have been unhappy with GEB since the mid-1970s, when he was told of GEB's dalliance with a young woman. Lim Soo Peng, a long-time friend of his, confirmed this. He told the author he was surprised that personal matters, rather than professional ability, should be of concern to the leadership. As far as he knew, it did not hamper GEB at work, even though it might not give the best impression of senior civil servants.

Friends and ex-colleagues dropped hints of powerful cliques in the government and business circles who thought of him as too bold or too vocal. The Keppel buy, seen as ill-judged and ill-timed, was the final denouement. Said Ang Kong Hua: "Generally, there was a view in the market that the Government should replace him because of the bad investment. And that was a view from the market, the corporate world. The fact is that he didn't want to step down; he wasn't asking to step down."

When Hon Sui Sen died in office in 1983, GEB lost his biggest backer in the government. Tony Tan, a former OCBC banker, took over his finance portfolio, which was later passed on to Richard Hu, head of MAS, in 1985. The former found himself having to answer a question from opposition politician J. B. Jeyaretnam about Keppel's fortunes. The MP asked whether Tan would make a statement on the acquisition by Keppel Shipyard of the shares in Straits Steamship. To this, he said there was no need to make a statement on a commercial transaction which was already reported in the media.

The events that led to GEB's removal are probably only known to a handful of people, especially those on the Directorship and

Consultancy Appointments Council. By 1985, he had relinquished his high-profile chairmanships, the last being his position at National Iron and Steel Mills. He dropped out of public sight.

There was another reason that could account for his absence in public life: declining health. By the end of 1985, he had chalked up one heart attack and three strokes. Whether these were due to the worries that had weighed him down or other reasons, it meant GEB was effectively out of action.

XII

The Last Decade

One of the people who stuck with GEB through thick and thin and through his final decade was Lim Soo Peng. The man who helmed the Chemical Industries conglomerate for most of his life till he stepped down from his chairmanship on 14 August 2020, had known GEB since 1952.

In fact, Lim could remember the very day they met. It was the first day of GEB's public service career when he was assigned to the Commerce and Industry Department. In 1952, GEB looked up Lim because he had been assigned barter trade as his portfolio and needed to write a paper for a delegation heading to Indonesia. The history graduate had no clue what barter trade with Indonesia, which would later become a source of acrimony between Singapore and Malaysia, was about. He alighted on Lim, whose family had been in the rubber business for three generations.

Lim, a former People's Action Party MP, recalled: "What does he know of barter trade? I had to tell him. He had no airs. He just wanted to know." They hit it off immediately and became firm friends for life, with weekly lunches, family visits and even trips abroad. In his letters to his daughters, GEB mentioned "Soo Peng" often, as "the old faithful" whom he shared "sorrows, successes and failures" with over the past 30 years.

Said daughter Paulina: "Uncle Soo Peng and Dad saw each other once a week. USP would send the car for Dad so they could have lunch in USP's office and there would always be gifts of fruit and fish … yes fresh fish, because of the nutritional value ascribed to omega oils."

When GEB retired from the Civil Service in 1981 on 31 October, just six days after turning 55, he was drawing about $6,000 a month, not much higher than the upper Timescale officers. He was then at Superscale A, which he had attained more than ten years ago. Higher-level staff grades were introduced in Parliament by then Minister for Trade and Industry Goh Chok Tong on 15 May 1979, and implemented in February 1981. GEB wasn't part of the promotion exercise, which moved up Sim Kee Boon, J. Y. Pillay and Ngiam Tong Dow. Thus, his pension would have come up to a little more than $3,000 a month. Younger daughter Christina said: "Sadly, his subsequent illness meant that he could not make up for his significant monetary sacrifices while in public service with a lucrative second career in business."

While he had non-executive appointments in what would now be known as government-linked companies, any remuneration he received depended on the say-so of the Directorship and Consultancy Appointments Council.

By 1985, he no longer held high-profile chairmanships. However, he continued holding on to some directorships, such as those at Focal Finance Limited and Lim's Chemical Industries, till his death in April 1992.

It was his good fortune that being a pensionable civil servant meant that he was entitled to medical benefits. He declined overtures from Keppel and Lim to pay his hospital bills, telling them that he would be able to afford them. When he died in the Singapore General Hospital, his children were told that the Pensions Department of the Accountant-General's Office would settle the bill.

Fiercely protective of his friend's personal life, Lim would not elaborate on GEB's financial circumstances. "He was my friend. That's enough. I don't have to explain to people how I spend my money."

Although she had never asked about his means of living, Christina maintained that her father was "by no means a pauper.... He sent me a monthly allowance, paid for my university expenses and airfares home, and willingly paid if I needed bus money, went out with friends." She described Lim as a "generous soul" whom her father would not like to offend by rejecting his overtures.

Lim set GEB up at the Marina House apartment at Shenton Way after GEB's divorce. When GEB became ill, he put him up in a Taman Serasi apartment near the Botanic Gardens and employed a live-in maid and a part-time nurse to see to his needs. The ground-floor apartment was convenient for GEB as he was, by then, in a wheelchair. Over the years, the big bluff man had become gaunt and pale, surprising long-time friends and ex-colleagues who visited him. He had trouble speaking.

When GEB got sick, his two daughters were in Adelaide, Australia. His son, then with the air force, was often away on missions. When she returned from her studies, Christina joined an advertising firm here. "I took a sabbatical from work to focus on his care after he had a stroke and was near the end of his life."

Paulina flew into Singapore each time her father's health took a turn for the worse. Along with her husband and three children, she flew back to Singapore for the funeral. So did GEB's sister, Patricia, and her husband. Michael, who was on official duty in Brisbane, took leave immediately when he was notified of his father's passing to be at the wake and funeral.

XIII

Staying Strong

The last decade of GEB's life is a tale of a man who was a legend in his time courageously grappling with the debilitating effects of a heart attack and three strokes.

His first heart attack in 1980 was something which Dileep Nair, who was his subordinate in the Finance Ministry, sometimes blamed himself for. It was an Old Rafflesian Association dinner that they had invited him to, and they "drank so bloody much and he went home and had an attack the next day," he told the author. But GEB recovered well enough to go back to work, continuing his tennis games with colleagues and friends, who called themselves the Morning Glorians, and making time to see to his responsibilities in Keppel and at the National Iron and Steel Mills, where he was chairman. Ang Kong Hua, who was then at NatSteel, said he showed no signs of any impairment or health issues. Work continued as usual.

In his letter to daughter Paulina in September 1984, just five months after leaving Keppel, he wrote to say that his doctor would be pleased with the "…old heart. I think that this is largely due to the fact that I am not so harassed now with the running of Keppel and have managed to cut my work down to an absolute minimum." He still had interesting and well-paid work with the British merchant bank Guinness Mahon and the New Zealand Milk Products, he assured her.

Two months later, he was even more chipper, writing that his blood pressure was under control, his lungs were clear and there was no indication of irregular heartbeats. "So you see, my giving up the chairmanship of Keppel has really done my health an immense amount of good. My only worry is that I have left Chor Teik [sic] and the boys to carry the brunt of the problems." Clearly, he felt for his friend Chua Chor Teck, the top executive of Keppel, who had to cope with the fallout from the Straits Steamship buy.

He spoke too soon.

In December 1984, he had the first of three strokes. It took place while he was visiting his sister and his daughters who were in Adelaide at that time. He was a fidgety patient, Christina remembered. "He was visibly depressed at being in rehab with people who were clearly much older than him [he was 50-something, they were white-haired 70-somethings]. When I visited him at the rehab centre, he would be dressed, showered, and sitting stiffly by himself, clearly upset and impatient to be somewhere else."

The second stroke in March 1985 gave him double vision and an unsteady gait. In October, he had a third stroke, which rendered him unable to walk and talk. He was laid out in hospital for 15 months before he could start walking with a cane and recover his speaking ability. As if life couldn't get worse, Chua Chor Teck died in January 1986. "Dad was pretty cut up. He and Chor Teck had spent a lot of time together and Chor Teck was a very special 'kinda' guy—Dad sometimes teased CT because everything was 'kinda'."

In January 1987, GEB was finally discharged from hospital. He had written to Paulina in December of the previous year to tell her that his doctor at that time, Prof Seah Cheng Siang, "agreed with alacrity ... must be 15 months was as much as he could stand of me."

"The walking stick is my weapon now but still confined to the house. With more practise, it should be okay outside and eventually for strolls in the evenings. But slowly, slowly catchee monkey," he wrote.

Christina recalled that her dad used to crack jokes about the doctor's mannerisms:

> I was often present when the Prof swept in to check on him. Famously, he would ask Dad to "Turn your head and cough." This became kind of a running joke with Dad and I. We would insert it into conversation as much as we could in front of the kindly Prof, who didn't seem to pick up that we were teasing him. Dad kept his playful sense of humour and used it to lighten the situation.

Likewise, his correspondence with his daughters through this difficult period was full of wry humour. He made sure to give them snippets of happenings in Singapore, tell of how friends were doing and how he was progressing health-wise. They were always upbeat and cheerful.

"He was usually thinking about how to improve his lot (re-learning to write, walk, etc), about some person who had visited, food he had eaten, a problem someone needed help with. His letters never reflected any self-pity," said Paulina. "His grumbles were not about his sad circumstances but the consequences of them—the 'damn' eyes that don't work like they should or the tiring exercises, or hurdles to overcome with even a simple trip away from home."

Christina said that even as his health declined, he showed tremendous strength of will, forcing himself to get up to do physiotherapy, speech therapy and practice walking. "In fact, he taught himself to write with his left hand when his stroke disabled his right hand."

His letters mentioned other friends who had stood by him besides Lim Soo Peng. There was lawyer Lim Choon Mong, the father of

Workers' Party MP Sylvia Lim. Lim was in the police force when GEB ran the Special Branch and was also one of the first batch of officers in the Singapore Armed Forces. There was his former colleague Tan Chok Kian, another Permanent Secretary of GEB's vintage. Both men would take GEB out for drives. "They are extremely kind and work on the basis that to be cooped up in a hospital ward all day must be 'soul destroying'. But stone walls do not a prison make!" he wrote in a letter to Christina.

Another close friend was Kartar Singh Dalamnangal, who would bring him chapatis and give him a leg massage whenever he visited him at home or in hospital. "He is always thinking of me and will ring me up when we have not met for some time," GEB told Christina. Son Michael shared that Kartar Singh, the man behind Kartar Singh Realty with an apartment block in Thomson Road to his name, shared "a deep but quiet friendship" with his father. "No histrionics and no banner waving. KS would come by quietly to Taman Serasi and massage his old friend's feet to provide comfort, then quietly leave when people started appearing at the house," he said.

By the late 1980s, GEB had moved from his Marina House apartment to the ground floor Taman Serasi apartment that Lim had got ready for him. A Filipina with a background in nursing, Myrna, was employed to care for him. Philip Yeo visited him once at Taman Serasi in 1990. There was a copy of *The Economist* in the apartment, about seven weeks old. After GEB indicated that he read the magazine to keep up to date, Yeo bought him a subscription.

Another visitor was Seah Kia Ger, who worked with him while in the Ministry of Interior and Defence and later in the Finance Ministry. He saw his old boss in 1990, 1991 and a few months before GEB's death the next year. It was "difficult", Seah said of the visits. The formerly strong, sharp-witted man could not raise himself from his wheelchair to greet visitors. Nor could he form a sentence to reflect what he was thinking. "I just talked to him about the economy, politics and what's happening in Singapore and he listened." GEB responded through gestures like thumbs ups and nods. Seah said he kept his last visit short as it was clearly taxing for GEB. Holding back tears, he said, "You can't find someone like him anymore."

Christina recalled acting like a watchdog when visitors arrived to see him in the Singapore General Hospital. Among them were the Keppel folks, who would wheel him to the window to look at Keppel Towers at Hoe Chiang Road, which was being completed. She added:

> Even when he was unable to leave his house because of his age and illness, he would get visitors all day, every day. It was like there was a revolving door. It was astounding. Men and women of all ages would come for advice, for a favour, for counselling, to exchange gossip, to say hello, to leave a special cake or favourite dish, to sit in contemplation, or talk about the old times. There was a notable pair of twin sisters in their 20s who adored his company. They would chatter on, bring him gifts and spend the afternoon having tea and cake. There was also a Eurasian lady he used to work with, much older than him, who would visit him every time she was in Singapore. She lived in Penang and invariably brought him a massive bottle of 4711 cologne and containers of pineapple tarts. The late President Wee Kim Wee also sent him packages of nonya kueh regularly, knowing that he liked them.

Talk to Lim about GEB's visitors though, and he would describe them as mere acquaintances and ex-subordinates, rather than the powerful who had benefited from GEB's help during their careers. Except for Lim Chee Onn, then a former minister who took charge of Keppel, and Herman Hochstadt, he couldn't recall any luminary visiting his friend during that time. With a tinge of bitterness, he recalled how his friend had never thrown his weight around even in his prime. People had asked for, and been given, favours. "All my life, I have never seen him talk down to anyone. Never mind that he was once head of the Civil Service, he treated everyone the same. But where were they when he needed their help? When a person is up, everybody gathers around."

His children saw things differently. Their father did not feel that "the high and mighty had deserted him," said Paulina. "His life was filled with people who made him feel needed. It is true that many visitors were hoping that he would still have the clout to help them but I know that he felt, that in spite of his dire straits, he was still of service to others."

His brother, Brian, a Catholic deacon, visited his brother every Friday morning to administer holy communion. GEB had also taken to reading the Gospels for a few hours a day.

Late in his life, GEB started keeping a record of his time during the Japanese Occupation, typing them on stationery bearing his name and address, a gift from daughter Christina. He managed 11 pages. "Typing this many pages would have been exhausting for him, and I think that's why he did about a dozen pages and stopped," she said.

Christina was there in his last hours and recalled:

> Eventually came the stroke that was so severe that he had to stay in hospital. When he became too frail to get out of bed, it was very hard for him. The day that he died, the doctors had met in the morning to discuss how he was doing. I remember that my Uncle Brian was there, but not who else or what was talked about. I decided to stay with him over the lunch hour, and am glad I did, for it was then he passed. I was able to comfort him until his breathing slowed and stopped.

George Edwin Bogaars died on 6 April 1992. For four days, his wake was held at a parlour in Singapore Casket. There were 12 obituaries published in *The Straits Times*, from companies and individuals. The funeral was held at the Church of the Holy Spirit at Upper Thomson Road.

The family was in attendance throughout the wake and funeral. Christina recalled some of the people who came:

I was advised to hold a long wake as there were so many people who wanted to pay their respects. I can't remember everyone who came. It was a big deal when Mr Wee Kim Wee came, with all his security people. He chatted with my mum for quite a while, he knew her well, used to tompang her [give her a lift] on his motorbike when they were younger. I also remember Charles Letts, who used to be in the British intelligence community and had a colourful past. Tay Seow Huah's widow and her son Simon came. Kartar Singh, of course, and his family. Lim Soo Peng was there the whole time, very distraught and in tears.

Michael recalled: "I saw a table full of rough looking individuals—tattoos and long hair—quietly sitting; they looked peaceful. A few tables further down sat some of the elite. It struck me what a wide and diverse span of people grieved his passing."

Lim choked back tears when he recalled how his larger-than-life friend had become a frail figure beset with misfortune. "He never had one unkind word to say about anyone," he added. "He was my friend, my friend. We were friends," he said. It was a phrase he repeated during the hour-long conversation he had with the author in the dining room of his Circular Road office.

In the room was an ornate grandfather clock. Lim had given it to GEB. On his death, his children gave it back to Lim as a keepsake.

Christina said: "I have the mantel clock with three chimes. I also have his small table clock which needs to be wound every day. It plays a wonderfully poignant tune for morning wake up. It makes me cry whenever I hear it, so I don't wind it."

Epilogue

When I was listening to him speak, I realised that I could only do so because it was George Edwin Bogaars who had set up the Oral History department of the National Archives. It was an assignment from the late Cabinet Minister Goh Keng Swee. Yet it is an irony that both men didn't live long enough to tell all—either they couldn't or wouldn't.

GEB died in 1992, when the department was 13 years old. It was set up to record personal, verbal accounts of people who can help piece together the country's history through their experience and knowledge.

GEB recorded his oral history interview in July 1980, among the first to do so. There are 43 reels of recordings bearing his name but only 13 are available for public circulation. It seems odd to me that a historian like him would want to keep historical material from wider public dissemination. Perhaps, there was a national security consideration because he talked about the days when Singapore was part of Malaysia and the setting up of the armed forces.

According to the National Archives of Singapore, GEB had "the sole right to permit use of his interview.... And he kept those rights when he passed away in 1992, as he wanted the interview interpreted in a way he personally approved. These terms are documented in a written agreement that the Oral History Centre is bound to honour.

If you agree not to cite, quote or paraphrase from the interview, we will allow you to listen to the interview onsite at the Archives Reading Room premises."

Without contravening those terms, I will just give a general example of how generations would have benefited from his account: How he, as head of Special Branch, viewed his work during the Confrontation period when Indonesian saboteurs exploded bombs in Singapore. You can check out Reel 27 under the Public Service series, provided you ask for permission first.

In a 16 June 1985 interview with the *Singapore Monitor*, when he had more time on his hands, GEB was asked if he would be writing his own memoirs for public consumption. He gave an unequivocal no. "There are two reasons for not writing," he said. "I'm a lazy person. To write, you have to put mind to paper. But if someone wants to write a biography or interview me, then it's OK, but for me to sit down and write, that's out of the question."

The other reason had to do with his father. When a foreign journalist wanted to write a biography of Sir Shenton Thomas, he approached the Bogaars family for documents that GEB Senior might have left behind that could give some insight into the man. GEB realised that his father, who was a confidential secretary to Shenton Thomas in the colonial days, didn't keep any. "My father was a stickler for form, he believed it was wrong for civil servants to keep documents. He didn't write because he felt it was wrong for civil servants to discuss official matters."

Like his father, GEB kept no official documents, his daughters said when asked if they found any in his house after his death.

Goh Keng Swee, who is credited for being the country's economic czar, didn't write his own Singapore story. Yet in every accounting of Singapore's history by any Singapore pioneer, he loomed large. It was fortunate that enough people knew of Dr Goh, who died in 2010, to write his memoirs. There are at least seven portraits and paeans of the man and his life-long achievements.

But Goh Keng Swee was a politician whose sayings and doings have always made it into the public record. Bogaars, on the other hand, was a civil servant who worked in the shadows, eschewing the limelight. The present generation would be more familiar with names such as Sim Kee Boon (died in 2007) and Ngiam Tong Dow (died in 2020). But they would be hard pressed to recognise names such as Stanley Stewart and Pang Tee Pow, backstage hands who put in place the Singapore story while the politicians went on stage. Death claimed them much earlier. They have since faded from memory, mentioned sparingly in the memoirs of others who had interacted with them.

For me, it was a pleasant surprise to unearth the man bearing the Bogaars name, someone whom I have always known was a "big shot", but without accompanying details. I don't believe I have come across such a colourful, charismatic personality who had such a major part to play in the nation's history—and who had left so little behind for future generations to peruse.

He did not fit any stereotype of the bureaucrat. He was sharp, yet blunt. He spoke his mind but could keep his counsel. He knew the importance of understanding politics but refused to be drawn into anything partisan. Despite being practically dragooned into the Civil Service by his father, he climbed to the top of the Civil Service tree.

He had some convictions about what being a civil servant meant.

In the early days of Singapore, it was about being oriented towards the needs of a new country and helping the people prosper. To do so required a certain alignment with the mission of the elected representatives, which was then a new experience for the former colony. GEB recalled that the priorities of the time were all about political security and economic development, which left civil servants breathless in the hurry to make sure a fledgling Singapore could stand on its own two feet. The pioneers were tough men who made tough decisions, and that sureness of attitude and vision aroused the admiration of their younger counterparts.

Philip Yeo, no slouch of a civil servant himself, described the first generation of senior civil servants as strong personalities who were more concerned about getting the job done than weighing themselves down with nitty-gritty paperwork and micro-management. It would probably be anathema these days not to go through the right processes. "Do you think that generation talked to ministers the way civil servants do now? In those days, they were equals."

Recalling his dealings with the pioneer civil servants, Yeo described Sim Kee Boon as a "don't rock the boat" and "get things done" type; Hon Sui Sen, who later became a minister, was "diplomatic" and a "nice guy" with whom nobody could quarrel, while GEB was "tough, very firm in what he wants to do".

Ex-subordinates told of how GEB would stare out of his office window in a meditative mood, wondering aloud if Singapore would become one gigantic carpark or asking why a road had to be built as a loop rather than in a straight line. He would astonish them with his straight talk and set them in stitches with some particularly pungent remarks. While his wit could be biting, he was never perceived as patronising. At least two people who did not know each other had this to say about him: that he did not have an unkind word for anyone, no matter the circumstances he found himself in.

Later in life, after he stepped down as Head of Civil Service in 1975, he would have a different view of how civil servants should behave with their political masters. He wondered why, with the country now safe and prosperous, they acted with "mindless efficiency", too quick to do whatever was wanted of them. "The Civil Service today should spend more of its time and effort thinking and planning and evaluating proposals rather than spending all its time implementing decisions." He thought they should be proactive about discerning future trends to put forth a menu of policy choices for the politicians to choose from.

"When a minister or someone in authority or even a Permanent Secretary gets a junior civil servant to do something, he is not inclined to sit down and think whether there will be any repercussions and tell him when there are problems."

He also blamed the Civil Service for the results of the 1984 general election, which led to two opposition MPs voted into Parliament and a 64.8 per cent vote for the PAP. There were some hastily thought-out government policies, he said, adding that they were "too many, too fast and too severe". He did not mention them, but he could be referring to the Graduate Mothers Scheme and the proposal to raise the withdrawal age of Central Provident Fund savings from 55 to 60. "I feel there is a threshold of pain above which politically you would not subject people to. There were too many changes and we have become a laughing stock."

Having worked in three different political regimes, from the British, through Malaysia to independent Singapore, he kept in mind that the civil servants' constituency was the people of Singapore, whose needs and feelings had to be taken into account.

But it was also clear that this wasn't a man who hopped to attention when his political masters spoke. He had never given examples but had often lamented about how being vocal was a disadvantage for a civil servant. He said in an interview with the *Singapore Monitor*: "I think a public servant should never say anything unless he is no longer a civil servant; I mean publicly. I was vocal because I'd merely spoken about things which I should have spoken about publicly and not because I'm against anything." One example could be what he said in 1974, when he criticised the Civil Service as being "terribly overstaffed", in his capacity as head of the public organ.

His experience with communists and communalists had left him with a keen sense of Singapore's vulnerability and the need to tread a fine line between achieving political objectives and being a political actor. As far as he was concerned, the civil servant was a problem-solver.

"Oh yes, there were people like [K. M.] Byrne and Goh Keng Swee who felt going into politics was the more direct, the more challenging way," he said, referring to the pioneering civil servants-turned-politicians. "But I was not interested in taking part in politics. I did not regard politics as the sole factor that shaped history. Politics was to me a fairly unsavoury business. That was how I felt, and I have no reason to change my view of politics even today."

How did he feel about the practice of recruiting politicians among civil servants?

"Professor Cyril Northcote Parkinson of the famous Parkinson's Law, who was my tutor in the university, once said that to be a successful politician, you must first be a successful something. So if you pick a successful civil servant and make him a politician, fine. My only concern is that you must pick the right guy but not try to make an unsuccessful civil servant into a successful politician. And I am saying this because there are unsuccessful civil servants picked to become politicians. Parkinson's Law on politicians is, to me, as sound as his other law on economics."

Prof Parkinson wrote in a 1955 essay that "work expands so as to fill the time available for its completion". In other words, officials tend to make more work for each other.

While he didn't give examples of "unsuccessful civil servants" who became politicians, he did point out two who had made the switch and impressed him. They were Goh Chok Tong and Lim Chee Onn. They had minds of their own, he said, and were confident and unafraid to argue for what they believed in. At the time of the interview in October 1981, Goh was helming the Health Ministry and was also Second Minister for Defence. He became prime minister in 1990. Lim was the secretary-general of the National Trades Union Congress and Minister without Portfolio in the Prime Minister's Office, as well as the MP for Bukit Merah. He left politics in 1992 and became Keppel chairman in January 1997.

It would seem that save for a few personalities such as his mentor Hon Sui Sen, Bogaars wasn't too enamoured of civil servants who crossed into politics. It was as if they had forsaken the "priesthood", which was how he described the Administrative Service, the pinnacle segment of bureaucracy.

After retirement, he used the term "political" on civil servants—not in a complimentary sense. The older generation knew less about saying or doing the right things to get ahead in their careers, he maintained.

> Today, you can hardly say that.
>
> Civil servants are fully aware of what they must do politically to advance their careers. Lots of young people know the right kind of thing to do, the right kind of thing to say in public. They are very sensitive about the political and social environment. We were a little bit stupid in that we didn't realise all these things and we said, "All right, we are in the Civil Service, we have to be good civil servants, no politics," and this could have been to the detriment of our careers.
>
> But today the young civil servant really knows he has to join the Residents' Committee. He is in with the crowd; he is saying the right kind of thing. He is very aware. He is very sensitive about what is going on in the political environment. I don't say this is good, bad or indifferent. I just think it's there.

What would he have said about today's civil servants and the continued induction of civil servants into politics? He would probably have a lot to say but would name no names nor give examples.

In his oral history records, Leslie Fong, a former *Straits Times* editor who interviewed Bogaars several times, described him as

> …very courageous. He was straining to tell Lee Kuan Yew not to politicise the admin service and Civil Service to a point where civil servants cannot do their professional job in giving professional neutral objective advice to the political masters and not, you know, in any way turn the service into one of mindless efficiency and quite forgetting its constitutional role in the country.
>
> Civil servants should not only tell the political masters what they want to hear. It was the job of civil servants to say, "Look, sir, you want to practise this policy, it is my job to tell you that these are the consequences." To offer that kind of input, rather than "Oh, that's a good idea" … which I think he felt the Civil Service was beginning to do.
>
> Because you see, in any power game, you sometimes don't have to spell [things] out. You condition people's behaviour by the way you act and Lee Kuan Yew was all-powerful. And by the way he can berate a civil servant or transfer them out … the other perm secs will know: Okay, this is not good for my career. So it takes a courageous person to say, "I don't care".

Fong told the author: "I have a high regard for George and still see him as a model for the type of civil servants Singapore should have. He was politically astute and courageous when it came to speaking truth to power, precise and cogent in the way he spoke and wrote."

While GEB's presence could be awe-inspiring, no one could accuse him of arrogance or throwing his weight around. Herman Hochstadt described GEB as a "gifted natural-born leader" in his memoirs. "His lesser colleagues, wherever he went, seemed to follow him most willingly with due regard and respect for him as a person and not just for his position."

His ability to get on with all ranks was well known. Seah Kia Ger said he had a down-to-earth, colloquial manner of speaking. He recalled in particular one Teochew phrase GEB often used: "pak si buay zhao" to say that a civil servant is forever a civil servant. "This was how he led people. He used such terms that you will remember. Not about missions or objectives."

Bogaars himself labelled pride as the greatest failing of civil servants. "It is a block and you cannot get anything done if you are full of your own importance."

Perhaps, because of his open nature, people were not disinclined towards asking him for favours, especially in the days when he had the ear of the powers-that-be. Francis Seow, the lawyer who later became a well-known Singapore dissident, had asked GEB to put in a good word for him to Lee Kuan Yew. After he left the legal service to start his own law practice in the early 1970s, Seow got into trouble and was suspended from practice for a year. In his book, *To Catch a Tartar*, he described GEB as "my good friend". Unfortunately for Seow, Bogaars relayed a terse reply from Lee, who noted that Seow had already left "the protective umbrella" of the Legal Service. Both men remained firm friends and corresponded with each other after Seow, facing tax evasion charges, fled Singapore in 1988.

Daughter Christina said that whenever the family members were out in public, her father would "inevitably be approached by people whom I could tell wanted something done for them. Same for most of the visitors to our house and later when he lived in his flat. They usually came asking for a favour of some kind."

He was known as a powerful force who could get things done. When he asked someone if they would like to have this or that appointment, he had the pull to make it come through. It showed his immense authority. Herman Hochstadt said GEB had put his name forward for many Civil Service appointments. Former

Internal Security Department head Yoong Siew Wah dedicated his unpublished memoirs to GEB, whom he had worked with at the Special Branch when he was there from 1951 to 1968.

But he also had enough trust in subordinates to eschew micro-management. This was displayed during his chairmanship of Keppel as well as his various Civil Service postings. Dileep Nair recalled how he was aghast when GEB, his Permanent Secretary at the Finance Ministry, asked him to chair a committee to appraise executive officers despite his rather junior station in the Administrative Service hierarchy. "He trusted his subordinates. He would always try to build their confidence."

In the days when civil servants lived in fear of Lee Kuan Yew, he was seen as one of the few men who could be forthright with him. Dileep Nair remembered a massive shelling Lee Kuan Yew gave to the Administrative Service corps, including permanent secretaries, about the low level of English language employed in the bureaucracy. Lee displayed the bloopers that had been made and didn't pull his punches. The silence in the room was only broken when GEB suggested the recruitment of teachers from Britain. "No one dared to say anything."

I found it sad that a man who had such a key role in building the Singapore story didn't have a fairy tale ending. Instead, his health appeared to have rendered his tremendous experience and insights irrelevant or useless to Singapore's continued development. His reputation has remained an "inside" story within the Administrative Service, of whom he was among the first locals. It is a story built up by his own career history as a spymaster, his forthright manner, administrative elan and his role during the thorniest times of Singapore history.

Keppel appeared to be his undoing. At the conglomerate's 50th anniversary celebrations in 2018, his name was left out of Prime

Minister Lee Hsien Loong's speech extolling the high calibre of its chairmen past and present.

Bogaars' last public appearance was in June 1990, when he was invited to the "SAF at 25" exhibition at Paya Lebar Airport. Seated in a wheelchair, he was pictured along with four others from the first batch of People's Defence Force officers—Ng Kah Ting, Othman Wok, Ivan Baptist and Eugene Yap.

To those who thought his last few years were "sad", daughter Christina had this to say:

> They are viewing him through the lens of their expectations. He did not have a big house on Nassim Road, an expensive car and a millionaire's lifestyle as many government servants then (and especially now) have. But he never wanted those things. He spoke out against them.
>
> He loved other things: intellectual pursuits, reading, time with friends, correspondence and helping others (e.g. blood donations and charitable donations). He travelled when he wanted to. If he was interested in something, like cooking, clocks or yoga, he taught himself about it.
>
> He valued curiosity, education, and faith. He always lived simply and happily. He enjoyed his friends and got a kick out of his retirement. I think the expectation in Singapore is for elder statesmen to have some kind of glorified life after government service. He was perfectly happy. Hampered by his physical/medical condition, yes. Sad, no.

In 2015, people who knew him rallied around to sponsor the George Bogaars Professorship in History at the National University of Singapore (NUS) to ensure that he would have a permanent place in the Singapore structure.

More than 35 donors contributed $2.6 million to the fund-raising effort led by his friend Lim Soo Peng; Ang Kong Hua, Chairman of Sembcorp Industries Limited who used to be with National Iron and Steel; and Ms Pang Cheng Lian, who worked for Bogaars at the former Ministry of the Interior and Defence. NUS said that strong support came from Keppel Corporation, NSL, Singaporean business magnate Mr Ong Beng Seng, Temasek and the Treasury Coffee Club, which is also responsible for commissioning this book.

In a July 1997 *Straits Times* report, former National Archives director Lily Tan said that GEB once told her that history should not be written straight away: "Lily, in your position, you collect and you keep memories, keep data. Leave the interpretations to professionals."

I am not a professional historian but I hope he would at least agree that this book is a faithful representation of his life. It was my privilege to write this.

Family Tree

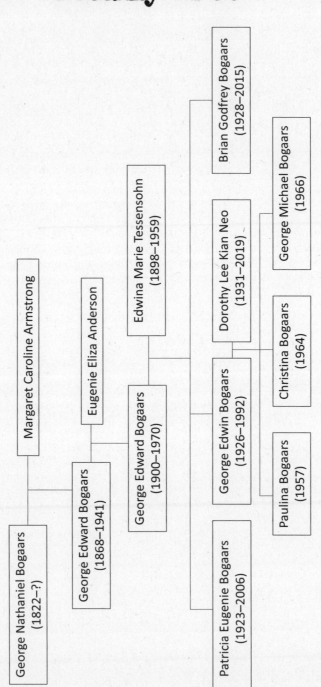

Sources

Many thanks to the following for their views:
Ang Kong Hua
Christina Bogaars
Michael Bogaars
Paulina Bogaars
Choo Chiau Beng
Barry Desker
Leslie Fong
Lim Soo Peng
Kishore Mahbubani
Dileep Nair
J. Y. Pillay
Ajith Prasad
Seah Kia Ger
Tan Siok Sun
Tay Kim Kah
Philip Yeo

ORAL HISTORY INTERVIEWS LODGED
WITH NATIONAL ARCHIVES OF SINGAPORE

Sheila Marguerite Balhetchet

George Edwin Bogaars

Leslie Fong

Bernard Tan Tiong Gie

Sim Cheng Tee

Kennedy Gordon Tregonning

DECLASSIFIED SPECIAL BRANCH DOCUMENTS, FOUND IN CHAPTER 5

1. DO/187/16: ISC (62) Draft Minutes of the 26th Meeting, held at Eden Hall, Singapore, at 6.00pm on Saturday, 8 September 1962.

2. DO/187/16: ISC (62) Revised Minutes of the 28th Meeting, held at Changi at 8.00pm on Thursday, 13 December 1962.

3. Selkirk to Secretary of State for the Colonies, 29 January 1963, CO 1030/1576, Telegram 53, p. 63.

4. DO/187/16: ISC (63) Draft Minutes of the 30th Meeting, held at KL at 4.30 pm on Friday, 26 April 1963.

5. DO/187/16: ISC (61) 22nd meeting, 30 August 61. Draft Minutes of the 22nd meeting held in Kedah Lodge, Cameron Highlands, Federation of Malaya at 7.30 pm on Saturday, 19 August 1961.

6. DO/169/20/58: Note of conversation between Mr Lee Kuan Yew and Mr Moore, held on 15 October 1963.

BRITISH DECLASSIFIED DOCUMENTS

1. Minutes from DO/169/538: Notes on Meeting between Singapore and Malaysian Government officials held on 19 May 1966, in the EDB Board Room (Chapter 7, pages 85–86).

2. FCO 16/199: Defence Policy: Defence Expenditure: Defence White Paper. July 1967 (Chapter 7, page 89).

3. Memorandum of Conversation: Mr George Bogaars, Permanent Secretary, Ministry of Interior and Defence, Mr Tay Seow Huah, Director, Intelligence Department, Mr Louis Sandine, Political Officer, Saigon and Mr E. L. Hickcox, Political Officer, 8 January 1968, Singapore (Chapter 7, page 89).

4. FCO 16/199: Defence Policy: Defence Expenditure: Defence White Paper. July 1967. Top Secret.

PRIVATE SOURCES

George Edwin Bogaars' personal collection
Yoong Siew Wah's unpublished memoirs

OTHER SOURCES

Newspapers
The Straits Times
The Sunday Times
The Syonan Shimbun
The Business Times
Singapore Monitor
New Nation

Magazines/Newsletters
Keppelite
National Iron and Steel Mills
Malaya: Journal of the British Association of Malaya

The New Eurasian
Management Development
Calibre

Government
Annual Reports by Keppel and National Iron and Steel Mills
Committee of Inquiry report on 1983 cable car accident Singapore
    Yearbook for 1974 and 1975
Television and radio programmes by Singapore Broadcasting
    Corporation and Radio Singapura, October 1967
Legislative assembly and parliamentary records
The Singapore Government Gazette

Websites
The Diplomat
Economic History of Malaya
Infopedia by the National Library of Singapore
National Archives of Singapore
Mothership

BOOK SOURCES

Abdul Rahman Putra Al-Haj (Tunku). (1969). *13 May: Before and
    After*. Kuala Lumpur: Utusan Melayu Press Limited.
Ang, C. G. (2009). *Southeast Asia and the Vietnam War*. New York:
    Routledge.
Baker, M. (2014). *The Accidental Diplomat*. Singapore: World
    Scientific.
Barr, M. D. (2014). *The Ruling Elite of Singapore: Networks of Power
    and Influence*. Singapore: Bloomsbury Publishing.
Blake, M. L., & Ebert-Oehlers, A. (1992). *Singapore Eurasians:
    Memories and Hopes*. Singapore: Times Editions.

Bloodworth, D. (2010). *The Tiger and the Trojan Horse*. Singapore: Marshall Cavendish International Asia

Bogaars, G. E. (1952). *The Tanjong Pagar Dock Company, 1864–1905* (master's thesis).

Cham, T. S. (2020). *Cham Tao Soon: Life at Speed*. Singapore: World Scientific.

Cheng, S. (1979). *Economic Change in Singapore, 1945–1977*. Southeast Asian Journal of Social Science, 7(1/2), 81–113.

Cheong, C. (2002). *Can Do!: The Spirit of Keppel FELS*. Singapore: Times Edition.

Chew, M. (1996). *Leaders of Singapore*. Singapore: Resource Press.

Chiang, M. (1997). *SAF and 30 years of National Service*. Singapore: Armour Publishing.

Chin, P., & Ward, I. (2003). *My Side of History*. Ipoh: Media Masters.

Chua, M. H. (2010). *Pioneers Once More: The Singapore Public Service, 1959–2009*. Singapore: Straits Times Press and Public Service Division.

Comber, L. (2008). *Malaya's Secret Police 1945–60: The Role of the Special Branch in the Malayan Emergency*. Singapore: Institute of Southeast Asian Studies.

Conceicao, J. (2007). *Singapore and the Many-headed Monster: A Look at Racial Riots Against a Socio-historical Ground*. Singapore: Horizon Books.

Desker, B., & Kwa, C. G. (2012). *Goh Keng Swee: A Public Career Remembered*. Singapore: World Scientific.

Drysdale, J. (2008). *Singapore: Struggle for Success*. Singapore: Marshall Cavendish International Asia.

Eurasian Association. (2015). *Our City, Our Home: Singapore Eurasians 1965–2015*. Singapore: Eurasian Association.

Hochstadt, H. (2020). *lives & times of hrh*. Singapore: NUS Press.

Hodgkins, F. (2014). *From Syonan to Fuji-go: The Story of the Catholic Settlement in Bahau in WWII Malaya*. Singapore: Select Publishing.

Huxley, T. (2000). *Defending the Lion City: The Armed Forces of Singapore*. Singapore: Allen & Unwin.

Internal Security Department. (2008). *Reflections: ISD at Robinson Road & Phoenix Park*. Singapore: Ministry of Home Affairs.

Kesavapany, K., & Pillai, A. D. (2019). *From Estate to Embassy: Memories of an Ambassador*. Singapore: Marshall Cavendish.

Koh, T., & Chang, L. L. (2005). *The Little Red Dot: Reflections by Singapore's Diplomats*. Singapore: World Scientific.

Kwek, S. C. (2019). *Resettling Communities: Creating Space for Nation-building* (1st ed.). Singapore: Centre for Liveable Cities.

Lau, A. (2003). *A Moment of Anguish: Singapore in Malaysia and the Politics of Disengagement*. Singapore: Marshall Cavendish International.

Lau, T. S. (1969). Malaysia-Singapore Relations: Crisis of Adjustment, 1965–68. *Journal of Southeast Asian History, 10*(1), 155–176.

Lee, T. H. (1996). *The Open United front: The Communist Struggle in Singapore, 1954–1966*. Singapore: South Seas Society.

Lee, K. Y. (1998). *The Singapore Story: Memoirs of Lee Kuan Yew*. Singapore: Times Edition.

Lee, K. Y. (2000). *From Third World to First: The Singapore Story: 1965–2000*. Singapore: Times Edition.

Lim, C. Y. (2017). *Lim Chong Yah: An Autobiography—Life Journey of a Singaporean Professor*. Singapore: World Scientific.

Lim, R. (1993). *Tough Men, Bold Vision: The Story of Keppel*. Singapore: Keppel Corporation.

Liu, G. (2005). *The Singapore Foreign Service: The First 40 Years*. Singapore: Editions Didier Millet.

Menon, R. (2007). *One of a Kind: Remembering SAFTI's First Batch* (2nd ed.). Singapore: Pointer.

National Trades Union Congress. (1973). *Towards Tomorrow: Essays on Development and Social Transformation in Singapore*. Singapore: Singapore National Trades Union Congress.

Ngiam, T. D. (2006). *A Mandarin and the Making of Public Policy: Reflections*. Singapore: NUS Press.

Peled, A. (1998). *A Question of Loyalty: Military Manpower Policy in Multiethnic States*. New York: Cornell University Press.

Poo, S. K. (2016). *Living in a Time of Deception*. Singapore: Function 8 Ltd and Pusat Sejarah Rakyat.

Pridmore, F. (1955). *Coins and Coinages of the Straits Settlements and British Malaya, 1786 to 1951*. Singapore: Govt Printing Office.

Ramakrishna, K. (2015). *"Original Sin"?: Revising the Revisionist Critique of the 1963 Operation Coldstore in Singapore*. Singapore: Institute of Southeast Asian Studies.

Sabnani, M. (2007). *More Than Mettle: The Keppel Offshore & Marine Story*. Singapore: Editions Didier Millet.

Sean, C. M. (1975). *Trends in Singapore*. Singapore: University of Singapore Press.

Seow, F. (1994). *To Catch a Tartar: A Dissident in Lee Kuan Yew's Prison*. New Haven: Yale University Southeast Asia Studies.

Tan, S. S. (2010). *Goh Keng Swee: A Portrait*. Singapore: Editions Didier Millet.

Tan, T. L., Tay, H. H., Pitt, K. H., & Leong, W. K. (2009). *Syonan Years, 1942–1945: Living Beneath the Rising Sun*. Singapore: National Archives of Singapore.

Thompson, S. (2014). *British Military Withdrawal and the Rise of Regional Cooperation in South-east Asia, 1964–73*. New York: Palgrave Macmillan.

Vasil, R. K. (2004). *A Citizen's Guide to Government and Politics in Singapore*. Singapore: Talisman.

Wee, K. W. (2004). *Wee Kim Wee: Glimpses and Reflections*. Singapore: Landmark Books.

Yap, S., Lim, R., & Leong, W. K. (2009). *Men in White: The Untold Story of Singapore's Ruling Political Party*. Singapore: Marshall Cavendish International Asia.

List of Sponsors

Ang Kong Hua
Chay Yee
Fong Seck Kong
Herman R. Hochstadt
Kuan Kwee Jee
Leo Lian Lim
Chris Liew
Lim Hsiu Mei
Lim Jit Poh
Jaya Mohideen
Dileep Nair
H. P. Mohd Noordin
J. Y. Pillay
Ajith Prasad
Seah Kia Ger
Henry Sim Cheng Tee
H. M Sithawalla
Tan Tee How
Keppel Care Foundation

Index